WHAT SHOULD I WRITE MY REPORT ON?

400 Thematic Research Ideas for Reports

by J. A. Senn

SCHOLASTIC
PROFESSIONAL BOOKS

New York • Toronto • London • Auckland • Sydney

Copyright ©1993 by Joyce A. Senn

0-590-49648-4
Designed by Vincent Ceci
Cover and interior illustration by Mona Mark
Cover design by Vincent Ceci
Printed in the U.S.A.

CONTENTS

CONTENTS

INTRODUCTION

During recent decades, knowledge and its many sources have grown at unprecedented rates—literally transforming the fundamental concept of what is worth knowing. Now the task of handling the superabundance of information available through the new technologies seems at best overwhelming and at worst—totally unmanageable and unteachable. However, unless students today are able to find the information they need, evaluate it properly, organize it logically, and present it in an interesting way, they will be unprepared to live successfully throughout the rest of their lives in this new Information Age.

Merely teaching the ABC's of report writing, therefore, is not enough for these Information-Age students. Before they ever get to put their pencils to a piece of paper, they now need to know how to find current information—as well as historical facts. For example, without any help, how many of your students could go to the library and find a copy of the food pyramid that the government recently issued? How many could find information about Hurricane Andrew in 1992 or get an up-to-date list of endangered species?

This book, therefore, provides many ideas for subjects that need research, but students do not have to actually write a formal report to show that they have found the necessary information. You could, of course, assign a report based on most of the ideas in this book.

The 400 non-report ideas in this book, however, have an additional advantage. Since all students do not express themselves best through writing, you will have many opportunities to allow some of your students to shine in their verbal or artistic skills. In fact, several times throughout the year, you may want to offer your students the option of choosing what form they would like to use to report information: writing, reading, drawing, or dramatizing. If you do, you may find that a group of students who would not get enthusiastic about writing a report might become eager participants in an artistic or dramatic project. Whether your students write a formal report, produce a timeline, or draw a series of cartoons, they will still be getting vital practice finding and evaluating information—a survival skill needed for the 21st century.

PREPARING

Before you actually have students select subjects from this book or assign them yourself, you may work with the school librarian to reintroduce your students to all of the resources not only in the school library but also in the public library. For example, if your school is still using a card catalog but the town is using a computerized catalog, then you need to plan a field trip to the town library so that your students can learn to access all of the information sources available to them.

Unfortunately most middle school students today can find only historical information—and mostly in encyclopedias—but it is more current information that is not only often more interesting to them but also more significant to their lives. You and the school and/or town librarian can show your students how to find information in such sources as newspapers, magazines, Facts on File, almanacs, and microfiche—as well as traditional sources such as non-fiction books, atlases, and dictionaries.

ASSIGNING TOPICS

Once your students feel confident finding their way around a library, then you can expose them to the ideas in this book in a number of ways. For example, you could generate interest in a certain broad topic such as "Robots" or "Outstanding Hispanic Americans" by reading the ten facts under each topic to your students. You may even want to involve your students in some discussion in order to assess their interest and basic understanding of a topic. (Your discussion, of course, could produce additional ideas for students to research.) Then you could hand out copies of a given topic and have your students choose which assignment they are most inter-

ested in, or you could simply assign one to each student.

The ten facts under each topic, of course, cannot possibly cover an entire topic. As a result, you might want to use the ten facts merely to get students interested in finding out more about the general topic. Then once they have done some initial research, they probably will find other facts that interest them even more than the original ten. If you take this approach, you usually will find that the students themselves will be able to come up with their own ideas for presenting their information—especially after they have become familiar with the different types of assignments covered in this book.

If some of your students choose to base their research on the ten facts under each topic, they should not, however, be limited to the two assignments under each fact. The assignments are merely suggestions, since there are many other ideas that would be just as acceptable and perhaps even more creative if they came from the students themselves.

ASSIGNING REPORTS

Once your students have researched their subjects and presented their information orally or in some other fashion, there is no reason why you could not also give them the opportunity of taking their information and applying it to a formal report—for an additional grade. Because they will have completed the hardest part of writing a report—the research—the actually writing of the formal report will probably seem somewhat easy to them.

You also may want to work with other teachers at your school to coordinate the use of this book with your students' other subject areas. It only makes sense that if your students do the research and then write a formal report about the Aztecs, for example, that they should get credit in English as well as in their history class if, indeed, they are learning about the Aztecs in that class.

USING CHECKLISTS

You may want to take the information in the following checklists and produce it in a larger format so that your students can refer to it as they do their research, organize their information, and possibly eventually write a formal report.

Checklist for Researching a Report
1. How many sources did you use to find your information? Did you use at least three?
2. If you used a card catalog—standard or computerized—did you look under more than one heading to find information about your subject?
3. If any of your sources are books, what are the copyright dates of those books? Did you check to see if there are any other books available with more recent copyright dates?
4. If your sources are all books, have you checked for more current information in newspapers and magazines?
5. Have you checked for current information in less standard sources like almanacs and Facts on File?

Checklist for Organizing a Report
(Following are different ways that you could organize the information in your report.)
1. Is your information arranged in chronological order?
2. Did you discuss your subject by comparing and contrasting it to something else? For example, did you state all the similarities together and all the differences together?
3. Did you make a statement and then prove it with facts and examples?
4. Did you present your information in steps that follow naturally one after another?
5. Did you state an opinion and then give reasons for your opinion?
6. Did you state a conclusion and then give the facts or incidents that led you to your conclusion?

Checklist for Editing a Report
1. Did you check for errors in grammar and usage?
2. Did you check for misspelled words?
3. Did you capitalize all words correctly?
4. Did you punctuate your sentences and the words within the sentences correctly?
5. Did you indent each paragraph?
6. If you quoted a source, did you quote it accurately? Did you use quotation marks around quoted material?
7. Are your footnotes or parenthetical citations written correctly?
8. Is your bibliography written correctly?
9. Did you use the correct manuscript form for a report?
10. Is your handwriting easy to read?

Checklist for Revising a Report
Format
1. Does your report have a beginning, a middle, and an end?
2. Does it have a clear thesis statement?
3. Does each paragraph support the thesis statement?
4. Does each paragraph move logically from one idea to the next?
5. Did you include transitions between ideas?
6. Have you included direct quotations and their sources?
7. Did you include footnotes and a bibliography?
Style
8. Do your sentences have a variety of beginnings and a variety of lengths?
9. Did you avoid rambling sentences and sentence fragments?
10. Did you use clear, concrete words?

AFRICAN ELEPHANTS

FACT 1

The average adult elephant is covered with about one ton of skin.

⭐ Write a poem about an elephant. Refer to its skin and tusks, two parts of its body that are very heavy.

⭐ Create a picture essay about the unique characteristics of another African animal. Include important information in labels and captions.

FACT 2

Because the average male African elephant is 10½ feet tall and weighs up to 6 tons (females up to 4 tons), it is the largest of all land animals.

⭐ With a partner, plan and tape record an interview between a reporter and an elephant. Explore the problems elephants have because they are so big and explain the elephant's solutions.

⭐ Create an illustrated chart that explains the differences between African and Asian elephants.

FACT 3

There are 40,000 muscles and tendons in an elephant's trunk.

⭐ Investigate all the different uses an elephant has for its trunk, and then explain in an oral report how other parts of its body—such as its ears and feet—are also well adapted for life in the wild.

⭐ Write and illustrate a children's story about an animal with another unusual physical feature—such as a very long neck.

FACT 4

Under normal conditions, African elephants in the wild would consume up to 500 pounds of food a day, and they will drink up to 40 gallons of water at a time.

⭐ Create a collage that explains the eating habits of elephants. Include important information in captions and labels.

⭐ Create a series of cartoons that illustrates the eating habits of another African animal.

FACT 5

A herd of elephants can easily cover 50 miles a day, walking at the speed of 5 to 5½ mph.

⭐ Draw a map that shows migration routes of African elephants. Also include the problems that elephants presently have following these migration routes.

⭐ Create a bulletin board that shows how captured elephants have served as beasts of burden in Africa and India in the past as well as in the present.

FACT 6 The very large skull of an elephant contains the largest brain of any land animal.

★ Work with others to plan and video tape a panel discussion on the well-established rules, regulations, and habits of elephants.

★ Give an oral report on how elephants communicate with each other and how they help each other.

FACT 7 Even though African elephants are so huge, they are among the most gentle animals, living in peaceful family units.

★ Write and illustrate a travel brochure to Africa. In one section, explain how elephant communities are organized.

★ Pretend you are a young elephant calf. In your journal, write a series of entries that explains what life is like as a young African elephant.

FACT 8 Today, African elephants are endangered. In Kenya alone, their numbers have been reduced from 150,000 to 30,000 in just the past 10 years.

★ Write and video tape a TV public service announcement in which you explain why elephants are being killed and what is being done to prevent their extinction.

★ Plan and dramatize a TV program for a nature series about another endangered animal.

FACT 9 Elephants have been used in circuses for at least 2,000 years.

★ Write an editorial for your school newspaper in which you agree or disagree with the use of elephants and other animals in circuses.

★ Pretend you work for a nearby zoo. Write and illustrate a booklet that explains the role that your zoo and other zoos are playing to protect elephants and other endangered species.

FACT 10 The closest relatives of today's elephants were the woolly mammoths that died out about 10,000 years ago.

★ Create a slide show about these early ancestors of elephants. Then record a narration to go with each slide.

★ Write a newspaper article on the complete mammoth that was found frozen in Siberia.

FACT 1

Christopher Columbus (1451-1506) returned to Spain after his 4 voyages to the new world with gold, spices, parrots, plants, and native slaves.

⭐ Draw a map that traces Columbus's four voyages. Include captions with important information about each trip.

⭐ Write an editorial for your school newspaper that explains the change in attitude toward Columbus in recent years because of his treatment of Native Americans like the Taino Indians.

FACT 2

Although the truthfulness of his claim is seriously doubted by historians, Amerigo Vespucci (1454-1512) maintained that he discovered the mainland America in 1497.

⭐ With a partner, plan and tape record an interview between Vespucci and a modern day historian who wants to know about his background.

⭐ Write a summary for a PBS television show about Vespucci's second voyage and why the new continents were named after him.

FACT 3

Juan Ponce de León (1460-1521) was looking for the legendary Fountain of Youth when he discovered Florida in 1514.

⭐ Write and illustrate the first chapter in a book about Florida history. Include how Ponce de León discovered, named, and colonized Florida.

 Pretend you are Ponce de León. Write a letter home telling your friends about your discovery of Puerto Rico in 1508 and how you were the governor for a short time.

FACT 4

Hernando De Soto (c.1500-1542) became the first European to see the river that the Indians called the Mississippi, the "Father of the Waters."

⭐ On a map, trace De Soto's journey from Florida to his discovery of the Mississippi. Include captions with important information.

⭐ Pretend you are De Soto. In a series of journal entries, explain your involvement with the conquest of the Inca Indians in what is now Central America and Peru.

FACT 5

In 1577, England's Queen Elizabeth I called on Sir Francis Drake (c.1540-1596) to disrupt Spanish trade on the Pacific coast of America.

⭐ Write entries in the captain's log that show how Drake's ship became the first to sail around the world.

★ Write a poem or a rap song that tells the story of Drake's defeat of the mighty Armada Spain sent to invade England in 1588. (You may want to include the fact that fearing Drake, the Spanish called him "El Draque," the dragon.)

FACT 6 Even today, Roanoke Island is called the Lost Colony because no one knows what happened to the 117 people who settled there in 1586.

★ Write the background events of the Lost Colony in the style of a mystery story.

★ Work with others to hold a debate on the different theories about what actually happened to the Lost Colony.

FACT 7 In 1623, the Dutch bought what is now New York City from several Indian chiefs by trading goods valued at 60 Dutch guilders (about $24). Of course, in those days, $24 was worth what several thousand dollars would be today.

★ Pretend you are Henry Hudson. Write what you might have said at a press conference after your "accidental" discovery of the Hudson River.

★ Create a timeline that explains the major events in the 50-year control the Dutch had along the Hudson River until they were defeated by the English in 1664.

FACT 8 The Pilgrims who came over on the Mayflower probably would have died if it had not been for an Indian named Squanto.

 ★ Pretend you are one of these early Pilgrims. Write a letter back home that tells all about Squanto and the things he did to help you and the other Pilgrims.

★ Write and illustrate a children's book about the Pilgrims. Explain their history before coming to the New World.

FACT 9 During the 1630s, about 20,000 Puritan refugees from England founded Boston, Salem, and the Massachusetts Bay Colony under Gov. John Winthrop.

★ Create a picture essay that explains what early colonial life was like.

★ Work with others to write and act out a short play that explains why Roger Williams and Thomas Hooker left Massachusetts. Also include where they went.

FACT 10 According to tradition, 12-year-old Princess Matoaka (nicknamed Pocahontas) threw her arms around Captain John Smith just as he was about to be clubbed to death.

★ Write and illustrate a children's biography of Pocahontas.

★ Record a guided tour of Jamestown, the first permanent English colony in the New World. Include an interview with Captain John Smith, Jamestown's first president.

ANIMAL MYTHS

MYTH 1
Bats are blind.

⭐ Pretend you are a bat. Then—from your point of view—explain to a group of young bats how they can use their ears and voices—as well as their eyes—to see at night.

⭐ Write a letter to the editor of your local newspaper. In your letter, defend bats and explain why they are so often misunderstood.

MYTH 2
Wolves live alone.

⭐ Create a picture essay—including captions—that explain how a wolf pack works together. (Draw your own pictures or cut them from magazines that belong to you.)

⭐ With a partner, prepare and present an interview between a reporter and a wolf. Prepare questions that reveal the wolf's way of life within a pack.

MYTH 3
Porcupines shoot their quills.

⭐ Draw a storyboard for a commercial for a nature series in which you explain how porcupines use their quills to protect themselves.

⭐ Create a slide show about porcupines and their way of life. Either photograph your pictures or draw them. Then tape record an explanation of each of your slides.

MYTH 4
Camels store water in their humps.

⭐ Draw a series of cartoons that explains—in one way or another—why this is a myth, not a fact. In your cartoons also explain the difference between camels with one hump and camels with two humps.

⭐ Write an advertisement that tells all the advantages of owning a camel—especially if the readers live in a desert climate.

MYTH 5
Bulls get angry when they see red.

⭐ Write a newspaper editorial that speaks out for or against the ancient sport of bull fighting.

⭐ Pretend you are a bull fighter. Then in a series of journal articles, write about your experiences.

MYTH 6

Ostriches hide their heads in the sand.

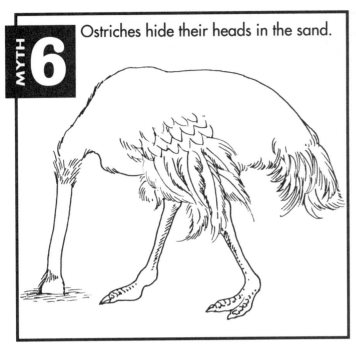

⭐ Write a poem or a song. In the first stanza of the poem—or the first verse of the song—explain how this fable probably got started. Then in other stanzas or verses, explain ways that other animals try to protect themselves.

⭐ Pretend that you are an ostrich. Then explain to the rest of the class the difficulties of being such a huge bird that cannot fly.

MYTH 7

Snakes bite with their tongues.

⭐ Write a newspaper article that reports on an incident in which a snake killed a raccoon. Within the article explain the function of a snake's tongue and tell how snakes actually kill their prey.

⭐ Show pictures of different kinds of snakes and verbally explain their unique characteristics.

MYTH 8

Raccoons always wash their food before eating it.

⭐ Pretend you are a mother raccoon. Write a conversation among you and your little raccoons in which you explain certain unique actions like dipping some food into water before eating it.

⭐ Write and illustrate a children's book about raccoons. Be sure to create an interesting title and cover for your book.

MYTH 9

A turtle can walk out of its shell.

⭐ Create a board game based on Aesop's fable of the tortoise and the hare. Part of the game should include fact cards that explain interesting features, habits, and characteristics of turtles. One card, for example, should explain why this myth could not be true.

⭐ Pretend that you are a tortoise. Write a letter to the editor of the Tortoise Gazette in which you express your frustration about always being confused with a turtle. Explain in your letter the ways in which tortoises are different from turtles.

MYTH 10

The owl is the wisest bird.

⭐ Write a fable that explains how this myth might have started. Within the fable, include some of the unique features of an owl.

⭐ Work with others to prepare and tape record a conversation among different forest creatures. The subject of their conversation should be the local family of owls and their habits and special characteristics.

ANIMAL TWINS

PAIR 1 — Rabbits and Hares.

 Pretend you are a rabbit—an ordinary one or a famous one like Peter Rabbit or Bugs Bunny. Then write a humorous editorial for the Rabbit Times, expressing your frustration over people always confusing you with a hare. Within the editorial, explain the differences.

 Some species of rabbits and hares are endangered, and some breed too much. Work with others to identify which species are which and then write solutions to both of these problems.

PAIR 2 — Frogs and Toads.

Draw a detailed picture of each of these creatures and then highlight the differences using lines and captions.

Some people think that frog legs are a great delicacy to eat. With a partner, debate the pros and cons of eating meat or being a vegetarian.

PAIR 3 — Butterflies and Moths.

Create a poster by drawing a large butterfly and a large moth, and then underneath each of them list their unique features.

Through a series of illustrations, show the stages a larva goes through to become a butterfly. Label your illustrations.

PAIR 4 — Crocodiles and Alligators.

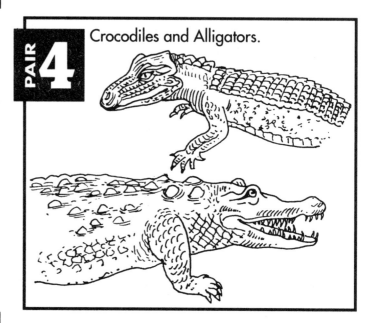

Create a comic strip that humorously explains the difference between these two animals.

For years alligators have been hunted and killed in order to make expensive shoes and purses from their skins. Work with others to plan a campaign of TV commercials and billboards to discourage the killing of animals for such purposes.

PAIR 5 — Seals and Sea Lions.

 Write and illustrate a children's story that explains the differences between these two animals. (Be sure to tell which of these animals usually are seen performing in circuses.)

Create a bulletin board that tells the story of the killing of baby seals for their fur.

PAIR 6 — Kangaroos and Wallabies.

 Write and illustrate a travel brochure about Australia that includes—among the unusual sights and attractions—kangaroos and wallabies. In that section, explain the differences between these two animals.

 Kangaroos and wallabies belong to a special class of animals called marsupials. Create a film strip that explains the unique aspects of marsupials and point out why they are limited to Australia and nearby areas.

PAIR 7 — Rats and Mice.

 Pretend that you are Mickey Mouse. From his point of view, write a speech that he might give at the National Mouse Association's yearly banquet. In the speech he should say that he cannot understand why people always confuse mice with rats. Then detail the differences.

 Write and illustrate a magazine article that explains the historical basis for the general fear that people have of rats and mice.

PAIR 8 — Dolphins and Porpoises.

 Create a mobile that highlights the differences between these two animals.

 Give an oral report on the superior intelligence of dolphins and their ability to communicate with each other.

PAIR 9 — Sheep and Goats.

 Write a fictitious interview with a sheep or a goat in which it complains about always being mistaken for the other. Then include the differences between these two animals.

 Create a bulletin board that shows the process of making wool, starting with the shearing of the sheep. Label each step.

PAIR 10 — Asses, Donkeys, and Mules.

 Pretend you are a cowboy. Write the speech you would give to a group of city slickers concerning the differences among these animals.

 Create a collage that explains why donkeys and mules are called "beasts of burden." Explain all that they do and why they are so good at it.

AZTEC EMPIRE

FACT 1 At its peak, the Aztec Empire covered roughly the same area as modern Mexico and included about 15 million people who lived in nearly 500 towns and cities.

⭐ Create a timeline that shows the development of the first Aztec settlements around 1325 through the construction of Tenochtitlan, the most powerful Aztec city. Include important information in labels and captions.

⭐ Create a filmstrip that explains the Triple Alliance that the Aztecs joined in 1426. Then show how the alliance totally changed their future. Record a narration to accompany it.

FACT 2 Aztec law covered almost every aspect of life including criminal behavior, divorce, land ownership, and even drunkenness.

⭐ Create a board game based on various Aztec laws and their punishments.

⭐ With a partner, plan and tape record an interview with an Aztec judge, who should describe the law courts.

FACT 3 The leader of the Aztecs was the Emperor, who was treated like a god.

⭐ Draw a diagram that explains the Aztec caste system. Then explain your diagram to the class.

⭐ Work with others to write and act out a short play that explains how people became slaves. Have the setting of the play be a slave market.

FACT 4 During one four-day Aztec ceremony, at least 20,000 people were killed in religious sacrifices.

⭐ Create a Who's Who of Aztec Gods. Write short descriptions of all of the major gods and explain why the Aztecs thought they needed human sacrifices.

⭐ Draw a picture of the Great Temple at Tenochtitlan and write descriptions of the important places in it.

FACT 5 The Aztecs used, and even often provoked, any excuse to start a war.

⭐ Pretend you are an Aztec farmer who hears the great war drum. In your journal, explain why the Aztecs were so eager to go to battle and why you are willing to fight even though you will not be paid.

⭐ Create a poster that describes and illustrates the three main orders of knights and their weapons.

FACT 6

The Aztecs did not have an alphabet, but they wrote in pictures called glyphs.

☆ Plan a demonstration of the Aztecs' use of glyphs and their use of codices, a type of book.

☆ Create a storyboard in which you explain how the Aztecs made paper.

FACT 7

Meat was a luxury in the Aztec diet, but when they did eat meat, they often enjoyed eating dogs. In fact, most families raised and fattened small hairless dogs to eat at special feasts.

☆ Create a bulletin board that features the diet of the Aztecs. Also include the differences in eating habits among the classes.

☆ Create a collage that highlights the importance of corn in the Aztec diet. Use labels and captions to include important information.

FACT 8

The Aztecs had two calendars: a solar calendar (like modern calendars) and a sacred calendar.

☆ Pretend you are an Aztec teacher. Give a talk explaining the solar calendar to a group of young Aztec children.

☆ Give an oral report that highlights the uses of the sacred calendar and explains how the two calendars worked together.

FACT 9

When Montezuma, the last Emperor of the Aztecs, heard about Cortes's arrival, he believed that Cortes was the god Quetzalcoatl.

☆ In a story-like fashion, tell the legend of Quetzalcoatl and explain why Montezuma thought Cortes was this god.

☆ Pretend you are Cortes. In a series of diary entries, explain who became your allies in the overthrow of Montezuma and tell about Montezuma's big mistake.

FACT 10

Within two years of Cortes's landing in Mexico, the mighty Aztec civilization was utterly destroyed.

☆ Write a comic book which explains Cortes's defeat of Tenochtitlan.

☆ Choose items for a time capsule that would explain (years later) what happened to Cortes after his victory and what happened to the Aztec Empire 50 years after Montezuma's defeat. Explain the importance of the items in labels.

THE BODY

FACT 1

Humans can survive a few minutes without oxygen, a few days without water, and a few weeks without food.

⭐ Write instructions for a survival kit that explains why the body cannot survive without oxygen.

⭐ Give a demonstration of CPR and teach others how to do it.

FACT 2

It takes blood about 23 seconds to make a complete trip through the body.

⭐ Work with two other students to plan and hold a panel discussion in which you explain how blood feeds cells, another student tells how blood cleans cells, and the third student explains how blood works to keep cells healthy.

⭐ Draw an internal view of the body that shows how all of the veins, arteries, and capillaries connect. Then explain your drawing to the class.

FACT 3

People have about 10,000 taste buds in their mouths and throats.

⭐ Pretend you are the food editor for your local newspaper. In an article, report on how the tongue, nose, and brain are all needed to taste food.

⭐ Give a demonstration of the four major kinds of taste buds. Then show on a diagram where they are located.

FACT 4

People's skin weighs twice as much as their brains.

⭐ Pretend you are a detective. Then video tape an explanation of how fingerprints are used to solve crimes. Use visual aids to make your explanation easy to understand.

⭐ Write an editorial for your school newspaper that explains why people have different colored skin. Then state the reasons why you think skin color should not be the basis for prejudice or discrimination.

FACT 5

A few people lose their second set of teeth and grow a third set.

⭐ Work with others to plan, write, and act out a skit for a public service announcement for children. In the skit explain how cavities are formed and what the children can do to prevent them. (You may want to develop characters such as Mr. Cavity and Ms. Toothbrush.)

⭐ Pretend you are a dentist. Then write the speech you would give your patients on the proper care of teeth.

FACT 6

After a person swallows, food takes from 4 to 8 seconds to reach the stomach.

⭐ Create a bulletin board that explores why people's stomachs rumble when they are hungry, and why certain foods make their mouths water.

Create a poster that shows what happens to food once it is swallowed. Include important information in captions.

Muscles make up about half of a person's body weight.

 Create a picture essay that explains why people need muscles. Be sure to add a caption to each picture you draw.

Write a personal letter to a friend or a grandparent in which you explain what a "charley horse" is, how you got one, and how you got rid of it.

FACT 8 The adult human body is made up of 100 trillion (100,000,000,000,000) cells.

 Create a timeline that illustrates how cells change and divide.

Create a glossary that defines and illustrates the different kinds of cells. Also include an explanation of the special job each kind of cell does.

FACT 9 A heart beats more than 36 million times a year.

Create a Valentine that includes information on how the heart works.

Pretend you are a doctor. Write a speech to heart attack patients that first explains how cholesterol can prevent the flow of blood through the heart. Then explain how to reduce cholesterol in a person's diet.

The normal human eye can tell apart about seven million different shades of color.

Create a collage of words and pictures that explains what it means to be color-blind. Then explain your collage to the class.

Make a diagram that shows how a camera works like an eye. Carefully label your diagram and include any additional important information in captions.

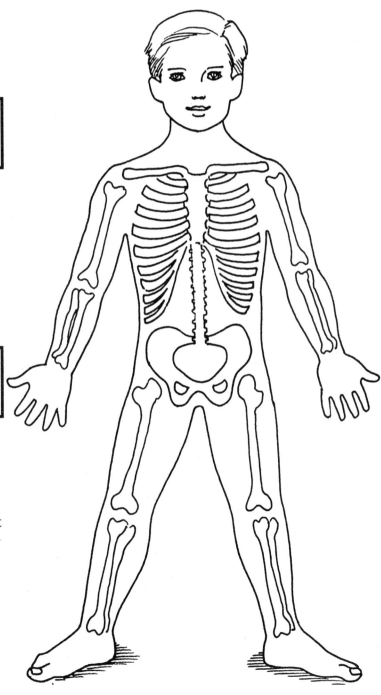

CHINA

FACT 1 One out of every 5 people in the world today is Chinese—in total over one billion people.

⭐ Create a poster that compares the quality of life today for Chinese in cities and in rural areas.

⭐ Pretend you are a Chinese student. Write a letter to a cousin who lives in America and explain China's policy of controlling the population by allowing families to have only one child.

FACT 2 Within China's boundaries lies Mt. Everest, the highest mountain in the world, and the Turfan Depression, which is 505 feet below sea level.

⭐ Draw an elevation map of China. Label it clearly and accurately.

⭐ Create a time capsule that includes items that reflect the great diversity of cultures within China's 21 provinces and 5 autonomous regions. Label the importance of each item.

FACT 3 China is not the world's oldest civilization, but it does have the longest continuous historical record of any society in the world—covering over 4,000 years.

⭐ Make a timeline of Chinese history, high-lighting the various dynasties and their rulers. Begin with the Xia Dynasty in approximately 1953 B.C. and include some information about each dynasty.

⭐ Choose one dynasty and tell about it in a story-like way to the class.

FACT 4 The Great Wall of China took 1,700 years to complete, and enough stone was used to build an 8-foot wall around the whole world at the equator.

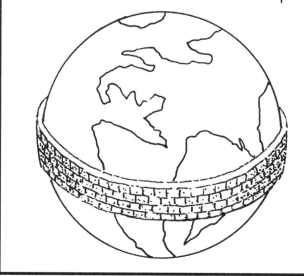

⭐ Produce a film strip that covers the history of the wall, beginning in the 3rd century B.C. Then record a narration to go with it.

⭐ Write and illustrate a tourist leaflet that includes interesting facts about the wall, including the different theories about why the wall was built in the first place.

FACT 5 Ts'ai Lun, an official with the imperial court, invented paper in 105 A.D., which was many centuries before paper became known in the West.

⭐ Create a mobile that features other Chinese inventions like the compass, porcelain, wheelbarrows, clocks, playing cards, the printing press, and kites.

⭐ Plan a show-and-tell—using pictures—to show how the Chinese made silk, an invention they kept secret for many years.

FACT 6 There are more than 50,000 symbols in the Chinese written language.

☆ Draw a comic strip that explains the different stages the Chinese written language went through as it developed.

☆ Work with others to plan and hold a panel discussion that examines the similarities and differences between modern Chinese schools and American schools.

FACT 7 The classic Chinese table is round to allow guests to be at equal distances from the food.

☆ With a partner, plan and tape record an interview between an American reporter and a Chinese chef. Include information about the basic diet of the Chinese.

☆ Give a demonstration of the use of chop sticks and show or explain the way much Chinese food is prepared.

FACT 8 Ping-Pong may be considered the national sport of China since so many Chinese play it.

☆ Create a picture essay that features other traditional Chinese games and hobbies. Also cover the Chinese's love of crickets and birds. Include important information in labels and captions.

☆ Give an oral report about the Chinese tradition of Tai ji quan.

FACT 9 According to an ancient legend, the Chinese allow a monster to come out of a mountain once a year during the Chinese New Year celebrations. However, they set off firecrackers to scare him away from their homes.

☆ Pretend you are visiting China during the Chinese New Year. Write a letter home that tells about this holiday and its other traditions.

☆ Write and illustrate a magazine article that explains another Chinese holiday, Liberation Day.

FACT 10 When China became a communist country in 1949, the Chinese people were not allowed to practice any religion, but this policy was changed in 1982.

☆ Write and illustrate a story that tells about the early influences of Confucius and Lao Zi on the Chinese.

☆ Create a bulletin board on Buddhism, the religion of most modern Chinese.

CONTINENTS

FACT 1 Before Leif Ericson or Christopher Columbus ever set foot in North America, a Norwegian named Eric the Red sailed to Greenland and set up a colony here.

⭐ Work with others to plan and video tape a panel discussion about the reasons why so many people—starting with Eric the Red—have settled in the U.S. and Canada over the years.

⭐ Create a storyboard that traces the steps of a family migrating to America in the early 20th century through Ellis Island.

FACT 2 Over 300 years ago, Sir Francis Drake first pointed out that the shapes of the coastlines of some continents seem to match the shapes of others.

⭐ Using a globe as a prop, prepare and give a speech in which you explain the theory of continental drift.

⭐ Create a poster in which you explain migration to North America from Asia over land that is now the Bering Strait.

FACT 3 Asia, the largest of all continents, is the home of more than half of the world's population.

⭐ Draw a map of Asia that reflects the changes that occurred there when the Soviet Union was officially disbanded on Dec. 25, 1991. Then write an explanation of the changes to accompany your map.

⭐ Create a photo essay on one of the three major religions practiced in Asia: Hinduism, Buddhism, or Islam.

FACT 4 Asia has some of the world's coldest and hottest climates, longest rivers, highest mountains, and largest deserts.

⭐ Draw a physical map that uses different colors to depict the elevations of different land masses in Asia. (Include a scale.)

⭐ Write a true story about Sir Edmund Hillary and Tenzing's successful efforts to climb Mt. Everest, which is not only the highest mountain in Asia but also the highest mountain in the whole world.

FACT 5 Africa, the world's second largest continent, is the only continent that lies in all four hemispheres.

⭐ Draw a map that includes all the continents. Highlight Africa's position in all four hemispheres.

⭐ Present a show-and-tell on the unique art that has come out of Africa over the years.

FACT 6 — Antarctica is the highest continent, with an average elevation of 8,000 feet.

⭐ Pretend you are stationed in Antarctica. Write a letter home to your family that describes your observations of what life is like on the tundra.

⭐ Write and illustrate a children's story that explains how polar bears and other animals are able to adapt to very cold climates.

FACT 7 — In the 18th century, England sent 170,000 convicts to colonize Australia.

⭐ Pretend you were one of these convicts. In your journal, write about the other inhabitants of Australia at that time, the aborigines.

⭐ Create a bulletin board of the unusual birds and animals that are found in Australia. Also include an explanation of why these birds and animals only live in Australia.

FACT 8 — Europe—with a population of about 500,000,000 people—is one of the most crowded places on the earth.

⭐ Give an oral presentation about Europe, based on a series of maps—including different maps for population, land use, ecosystems, climate, and physical features.

⭐ Write and illustrate a travel brochure that gives information about the major cities in Europe.

FACT 9 — In Argentina and other South American countries south of the equator, it is summertime during the months of Dec., Jan., and Feb.

⭐ Make a chart that compares South America to all of the other continents in such areas as size, population, natural resources, etc.

⭐ Create a board game about some of the major cities in South America.

FACT 10 — The distance between the Caribbean Sea and the Pacific Ocean is only 48 miles through the Panama Canal.

⭐ With a partner, plan and tape record an interview with the director of the Panama Canal. In the interview, concentrate on the building of the canal.

⭐ Give an oral report that explains why the Panama Canal was once so important to the U.S. and why that importance has declined in recent years.

DESERTS

FACT 1

Nearly one third of the land on the earth is covered by deserts.

⭐ Draw a map that highlights all the major deserts of the world. At the top of the map, include a definition of a desert.

⭐ Write and illustrate a chapter in a children's geography book in which you explain the difference between tropical deserts and cold deserts. Give examples of each kind.

FACT 2

The Sahara Desert is the largest desert in the world. In fact, it is almost as large as the entire U.S.

⭐ Write an article for a nature magazine that explains desertification, or why deserts are getting bigger. At the end of your article, offer some solutions to this problem.

⭐ Create a chart that explains the unique aspects of the Sahara Desert and other major deserts—such as the Painted Desert in Arizona, the Gobi Desert in Mongolia, and the Great Australian Desert.

FACT 3

The town of Tidikelt in the Sahara once went 10 years without a rainfall.

⭐ Work with others plan and hold a panel discussion on the different reasons why deserts are so dry.

⭐ With a partner, plan and tape record an interview between a reporter and an expert on deserts. During the interview, discuss what phantom rain is and explore why some moisture in the desert air turns to fog, not rain.

FACT 4

Tens of thousands of years ago, the Sahara regions were covered with green vegetation and filled with wildlife.

⭐ Write an editorial for your local newspaper in which you compare the Sahara tens of thousands of years ago to the rainforests now in South America.

⭐ Write and illustrate a travel brochure for the Sahara. In it, tell about oases—how they exist in a desert and how long they last.

FACT 5

The Bedouins of the Arabian peninsula have made the desert their home for many centuries.

⭐ Pretend you are a Bedouin child. In your diary, write about life in the desert.

⭐ Create a bulletin board that shows how people living in or around deserts are contributing to *desertification*. Also offer some solutions to this problem.

FACT 6

The saguaro cactus of Arizona and New Mexico expands like an accordion to take in water during the few rains of the year.

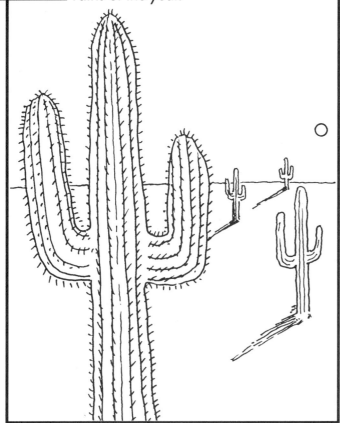

⭐ Write a booklet called "Surviving in the Desert." In it, explain how plants like cacti, which are also called *xerophytes*, survive in the desert.

⭐ Create an illustrated chart that shows the differences between *xerophytes* and *ephemeral* plants.

FACT 7

Animals that cause terrible problems in several deserts are goats.

⭐ Write an article for the Goat Gazette in which you explain how goats got into the desert in the first place and what kinds of damage they are doing.

⭐ Create a glossary of animals and insects that live in the desert. If possible, also include an illustration of each one.

FACT 8

The first step in reclaiming part of a desert is anchoring the sand dunes.

⭐ Pretend you are on a vacation in Arizona. Write a letter back home and explain what you have learned about anchoring sand dunes.

⭐ Create a picture essay that tells about what countries are doing with land they have reclaimed from the desert.

FACT 9

The desert along the southwestern coast of Africa is noted for the mining of diamonds.

⭐ Create a film strip that explains how diamonds are formed. Then record a narration that goes along with it.

⭐ Create a storyboard that shows how diamonds are mined.

FACT 10

Borax, magnesium, sodium, phosphates, and a dozen other minerals used to make soap, water softeners, and a thousand other products have been found in the Mojave Desert in CA.

⭐ Write and tape-record a walking tour through part of the Mojave Desert. Describe things as if you were walking by them.

⭐ Write and illustrate a children's book called Life in the Desert.

EARTHQUAKES

FACT 1

Scientists locate and study more than 150,000 earthquakes every year.

★ Create a slide show that explains the 3 kinds of faults that produce earthquakes: normal, thrust, and strike-slip. Then tape-record a narration to go with each slide.

★ Create a poster that explains the 3 kinds of earthquake waves: primary, secondary, and surface.

FACT 2

A modern seismograph can record a tiny earth tremor thousands of miles away.

★ Work with others to plan and hold a panel discussion on how scientists use readings from seismographs to find an earthquake's force, its focus underground, and its epicenter.

★ Pretend that you are Charles Richter. In a series of journal entries, write about your invention of the Richter Scale and explain what it does.

FACT 3

The most deadly earthquake in the U.S. occurred in San Francisco, California, on April 18, 1906, leaving more than 500 dead or missing.

★ Present a picture essay about the 1906 San Francisco earthquake to the class. Use pictures you have drawn or show pictures from books as you tell about the quake.

★ Give an oral report on the reasons that fewer people are killed by earthquakes in the U.S now than were killed years ago.

FACT 4

The earthquake that shook the San Francisco area on Oct. 17, 1989 (during the World Series) measured 7.1 on the Richter Scale and X to XI on the Mercalli Scale.

★ Create a chart that lists the 12 points on the Mercalli Scale. Then find or draw pictures that illustrate each point.

★ Write a summary for a movie about the 1989 San Francisco earthquake.

FACT 5

About the only places in the U.S. that have never recorded an earthquake are the southern parts of Florida, Alabama, and Texas.

★ Draw a map of the continental U.S. and mark the 4 earthquake zones: none, minor, moderate, and major. Then give a talk explaining why most earthquakes in the U.S. occur in CA.

★ With a partner, write and tape-record an interview between a reporter and a seismologist. Include a discussion of the importance of the San Andreas fault.

FACT 6 The most violent earthquake ever recorded in the U.S. occurred on March 27, 1964, in Anchorage, Alaska. It measured 8.4 on the Richter Scale.

★ Write a story-like account of the Alaskan earthquake, but base it entirely on facts.

★ Write a newspaper article that covers another violent earthquake that hit Armenia in 1988, killing 40,000 people.

FACT 7 A deadly tsunami killed 3,000 people on the island of Honshu in Japan in 1933. The tidal wave also sank 8,000 ships and destroyed 9,000 homes.

★ Pretend you are an elementary school-teacher. Plan a lesson that would explain what a tsunami is and what causes it. Use visual aids to help your students' understanding.

★ Pretend you were in Peru in 1971 when an earthquake caused an avalanche. Write a letter home describing what happened.

FACT 8 Nine days after the 1985 earthquake in Mexico City, 35 people and 8 newborn babies were pulled alive out of the rubble.

★ Write and illustrate a magazine article telling about the earthquake in Mexico City in 1985.

★ Create a bulletin board that explains improved earthquake rescue techniques and tools—such as thermal image cameras and sniffer dogs.

FACT 9 In 1976, a city in China was evacuated on the basis of the behavior of the birds and animals in the area. Hours later an earthquake struck and reduced the town to rubble.

★ Pretend you are a Chinese bird expert. At a press conference following the 1976 earthquake, explain the Chinese theory behind using birds and animals to predict earthquakes.

★ Write a section for a children's science book that explains ways to predict earthquakes, including the "elastic rebound" theory.

FACT 10 In 1914, the famous American architect Frank Lloyd Wright designed the Imperial Hotel in Tokyo to be quakeproof. Three years after it was completed, Tokyo was hit by the worst earthquake in its history. Wright's hotel was the only building left standing for miles.

★ Pretend you are Frank Lloyd Wright. In a series of journal entries, explain your plans for making the hotel quakeproof.

★ Pretend you are a writer for Architectural Digest. Write an article that examines what has been done in recent years to make buildings more quakeproof.

EARTH REPORT

FACT 1 On April 22, 1970, the first Earth Day was celebrated. More than 20 million people marched in parades, sang songs, and attended teach-ins on the environment.

⭐ Create a picture essay about the first Earth Day. Include all important information in labels and captions.

⭐ Work with others to plan activities for a local Earth Day. Then send your ideas to the mayor of your town.

FACT 2 During 1970, the Environmental Protection Agency (EPA) was formed by the U.S. government to enforce laws that protect the environment.

⭐ Work with others to plan and hold a panel discussion on the work of the EPA and the laws it tries to enforce.

⭐ Find out what young people can do to help the environment by writing to Kids for a Clean Environment, P.O. Box 158254, Nashville, TN 37215. Also interview friends, family members, and teachers for additional ideas. Then report your findings to the class.

FACT 3 In 1972, the Clean Air Act identified the 6 most common dangerous pollutants: lead, sulfur oxide, carbon monoxide, particulates, ozone, and nitrogen oxide.

⭐ Write a newspaper article that reports on the most common ways that these pollutants get into the air.

⭐ Write to your state environmental affairs office to find out what air problems your state has. Then work with others to propose some solutions.

FACT 4 In 1973, the Endangered Species Act was passed to protect wildlife.

⭐ Plan and video-tape a TV program for PBS on one endangered species.

⭐ Draw a poster that urges people to protect endangered species. Include persuasive arguments to convince them.

FACT 5 In 1974, the Safe Drinking Water Act outlawed pollutants to ensure that drinking water is safe.

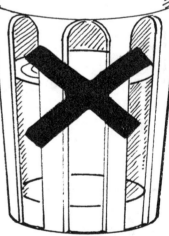

⭐ Create a question-and-answer newspaper column. Then write an answer to the following question: What is the background of the Safe Drinking Water Act?

⭐ Write a short story—based on facts—about what happens to a small town when its entire water supply becomes contaminated. End with what the town could have done to prevent such a fate.

FACT 6

In 1976, the Toxic Substance Control Act was passed to prevent farmers from using harmful pesticides to kill insects that damage their crops.

☆ Give an oral report that presents the progress of this act. For example, in 1993, farmers were still using some pesticides that are harmful to children.

☆ Work with others to plan and video tape a debate between farmers who say they need pesticides to make a living and consumers who are afraid of the harm caused by pesticides in their food.

FACT 7

In 1982, a hole was discovered in the ozone layer over Antarctica.

☆ Create a bulletin board that includes the problems that have already resulted and those that will occur in the future because of this hole.

☆ Pretend you are a TV reporter. Write and video tape a report on the finding of this first hole in the ozone layer.

FACT 8

In 1982, the EPA created a "super-fund," setting large amounts of money aside to clean up harmful waste sites.

☆ Work with others to write, rehearse, and present a one-act play that reveals what happened at one of the most famous contaminated sites, Love Canal in NY.

☆ Call your state environmental affairs office to find out if there are any harmful waste sites in your state. Then write to the EPA at 401 M Street S.W., Washington D.C. 20460 and find out what is being done with the site. Present your findings to the class.

FACT 9

In 1988, scientists discovered a second hole in the ozone layer—this time over the Arctic.

☆ With a partner, write and tape record an interview between a reporter and a scientist. Include the significance of the second hole.

☆ Write to The Greenhouse Crisis Foundation at 1130 17th Street N.W., Washington, D.C. 20036, and find out how the holes in the ozone layer may be contributing to global warming. Then after reading about the greenhouse effect, put your findings in writing.

FACT 10

On April 22, 1990, Earth Day 2 was celebrated. This time 100 million people around the globe participated.

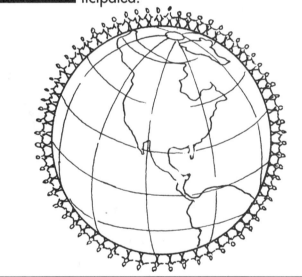

☆ Write an editorial for the school newspaper about the changes made since the first Earth Day. Then suggest ways to get people more actively involved in protecting the environment.

☆ Create a timeline that includes the major events listed in the 10 facts of this Earth Report. Then add the rest of your lifetime to the timeline, imagining what the future will bring—for better and for worse.

FACT 1

Indians, or Native Americans, lived in the Americas for approximately 30,000 years before any Europeans arrived.

★ Draw a map of the U.S. and mark in the areas occupied by major tribes. Include some unique aspect of each tribe.

★ Make a poster that shows the similarities among the different U.S. tribes.

FACT 2

The Iroquois were respected warriors, and their remarkable gift for democratic government was greatly admired by statesmen like Benjamin Franklin.

★ In an oral report, explain how the Iroquois nation was actually a league of 5 tribes, called the League of Peace, or the Great Peace.

★ Work with others to write, rehearse, and perform a short play that reenacts what happened at the Great Albany Congress in 1754. Include the impression that the League of Peace made on Benjamin Franklin.

FACT 3

On a cold November morning in 1683, an unarmed William Penn met for the first time with Tamanend, the chief of the Delaware Indians, to sign the Great Treaty.

★ Pretend you are William Penn. In a series of journal articles, discuss your attitude toward the Delaware Indians. Also explain why your treatment of the Indians was so unusual during that time.

★ With a partner, plan and video tape a conversation between Chief Tamanend and William Penn. Tamanend should explain why he made the treaty with Penn, and they both should tell what gifts they exchanged.

FACT 4

In the southeastern part of the U.S., the most famous and warlike Indians were five tribes known as the Five Civilized Tribes.

★ Write and illustrate a section of an elementary history book that explains which tribes belong to this group, why they were called the "civilized tribes," and how this group was different from the League of Peace to its north.

★ The largest of the five tribes was the Cherokees. Create a picture essay that tells about the traditions and legends of this tribe.

FACT 5

Grief stricken over the death of his third daughter, Hiawatha temporarily gave up his efforts to bring peace to his people.

★ Write and illustrate a biography of Hiawatha—or Deganawida—and explain his part in forming The Great Peace among the Iroquois nations.

★ Pretend you are Chief Tuscarora. In a letter to Hiawatha, explain why you first opposed the Great Peace. Then tell why your tribe finally became the Sixth Nation.

FACT 6 When the American Revolution broke out in 1775, both the colonists and the British tried to get the Native Americans' support.

☆ Create a timeline showing the major events in which an Irish man named Sir William Johnson influenced many Native Americans to support the British during the Revolution. Add important information in captions.

☆ Create a bulletin board showing the part that Joseph Brant (Thayendanegea), the war chief of the League of Six Nations, played in the American Revolution.

FACT 7 In 1821, Sequoyah, a Native American scholar, developed a Cherokee alphabet.

☆ Plan an educational TV show about the life of Sequoyah.

☆ Create a bulletin board that compares and contrasts the Cherokee alphabet with the alphabet we use to write English (the Roman alphabet.)

FACT 8 In the winter of 1838-1839, 60,000 members of the Five Civilized Tribes were forced to leave their homes in the East. During a journey known as the Trail of Tears, between 1/4 and 1/2 of them died before reaching their new home in the West.

☆ Write the story of what happened during the Trail of Tears and then read it dramatically to the class.

☆ Research what happened to Japanese-Americans during World War II. Create a display comparing and contrasting these events with The Trail of Tears, and any other similar events in history you know of.

FACT 9 After two unsuccessful wars with the Seminoles, the U.S. government allowed them to remain in the East; however, some Seminoles never resumed official relationships with the U.S. until 1962.

☆ Write and illustrate a chapter in an elementary history book that tells about the two Seminole wars.

☆ Pretend you are a descendent of a group of 1000 Seminoles who fled into the mountains of NC during the winter of 1838. Write and tape record a press conference you might hold now to tell what happened then and what that group of Seminoles is doing today.

FACT 10 Early in the 19th century, the great Shawnee, Techumseh, became the last Indian to try to unite the eastern tribes.

☆ Pretend you are an English settler during the early 19th century. Write an editorial for a local newspaper in which you explain the reasons for your and your neighbors' genuine fear of Techumseh.

☆ Write a poem or a song that explains what happened to kill Techumseh's dream of a single united Indian nation.

ENDANGERED SPECIES

FACT 1

The first U.S. list of endangered species was made in 1967; it included 78 species. The current list contains more than 1,200 species.

⭐ Write an educational leaflet on what criteria are used to place a species on the endangered list.

⭐ Create a timeline that includes all legislation that has been enacted to protect endangered species. For some help, you could write to the Society for Animal Protective Legislation, P.O. Box 3719, Georgetown Station, Washington D.C. 20007.

FACT 2

About 40% of all of Hawaii's native bird species have already become extinct.

⭐ Create a slide show about some of the unusual species of birds and animals in tropical climates like Hawaii. Then record a narration to go with each slide.

⭐ Work with others to come up with ideas for preserving the bird population in your city and state. Then send your ideas to your local newspaper.

FACT 3

Some scientists estimate that 10% of all species of fish are endangered.

⭐ Work with others to plan and video tape a panel discussion about the general causes of fish becoming endangered. Then offer some possible solutions.

⭐ With a partner, plan a debate about the problem of overfishing in places like Georges Bank off the coast of MA. One should defend the position of the fishermen and the other should defend the position of the consumers.

FACT 4

The average age of captive dolphins is 5.8 years, but the average natural life-span of free dolphins is 25 years.

⭐ Write and video tape a TV editorial that deals with the issue of keeping highly intelligent animals like dolphins captive in small areas just to perform for people.

⭐ Write a newspaper article about what the U.S. has done to save dolphins and whales from being caught in fishermen's nets. In addition to your own research, you could write to the Save the Dolphins Project (Earth Island Institute), 300 Broadway, Suite 28, San Francisco, CA 94133.

FACT 5

The mountain gorillas in Africa became an endangered species in 1931—only 31 years after they were discovered.

★ Write and illustrate a children's story about gorillas.

★ Pretend you are Jane Goodall, who has spent most of her life studying African chimpanzees. Write what you would say at a press conference to report what is being done to protect them.

FACT 6
In 1989, the General Accounting Office reported that only 16% of endangered species in the U.S. were improving their status, while 1/3 were deteriorating.

★ Create a bulletin board of all state and local species of plants, animals, fish, and birds that are endangered. Picture and label each one. (You could get some help by calling or writing to state and local environmental organizations.)

★ Work with others to plan a state-wide campaign to save endangered species. Include billboards, magazine ads, and TV commercials.

FACT 7
All species of rhinoceros are endangered.

★ Pretend you are a rhinoceros. Write a letter to the world in which you plead for your life.

★ Create a film strip that tells about another endangered animal. Then record a narration to go with it.

FACT 8
The Center for Plant Conservation predicts that up to 700 species of U.S. plants may become extinct by the year 2000.

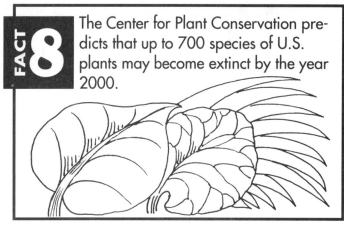

★ Create a picture essay that features some endangered plants and explains why they are important in the food chain.

★ Create a poster that shows how the extinction of plants in the South American rainforests will eventually affect people in the U.S.

FACT 9
In 1989, the General Accounting Office reported that only the following species have been removed from the endangered list: the American alligator, the Palau dove, the Palau fantail, the Palau owl, and the brown pelicans in the Southeast.

★ Write and illustrate a magazine article about one of these species.

★ Work with others to plan a backyard bird sanctuary at your school. You can get some help by writing to the National Wildlife Federation Backyard Wildlife Habitat Program, 1412 16th St. N.W., Washington D.C. 20036.

FACT 10
In the last 30 years, at least 300 vertebrate animals have become forever extinct.

★ Give an oral report on some animals that have become extinct in the U.S.—such as the Eastern buffalo or the Arizona jaguar.

★ Write and illustrate a children's story about one of the most famous extinctions—the Dodo bird.

FIRSTS FOR WOMEN

FACT 1
The first woman pilot to fly alone across the Atlantic Ocean was Amelia Earhart.

★ With a partner, plan and tape record an interview between a reporter and Earhart after her flight across the Atlantic.

★ Create a timeline that shows the development of flight. Include important information in labels and captions.

FACT 2
The first woman cartoonist who had a syndicated comic strip was Dale Messick. Her comic strip, "Brenda Starr," first appeared on June 19, 1940, in the Chicago Tribune.

★ Draw your own comic strip about the life of a famous woman such as Abigail Adams, Eleanor Roosevelt, or Sandra Day O'Connor.

★ Pretend you are Mrs. John Peter Zenger, who lived in New York during colonial times. Write and present a monologue in which she explains what happened to her husband. Include how that incident was a big step toward establishing freedom of the press in America.

FACT 3
The first woman pictured on a U.S. coin was suffragist Susan B. Anthony.

★ Create a picture essay—including captions—that highlights some of the main events that occurred in the suffragist movement.

★ Create a new coin in which you honor a modern woman. Then explain your coin to the class and give the reasons why you pictured the woman you did.

FACT 4
The first woman runner to win three gold medals in the Olympics was Wilma Rudolph.

★ Pretend you are Wilma Rudolph. Through a series of diary entries, tell what happened on your long road to becoming an Olympic winner.

★ Give an oral report that contrasts the ancient Olympic games with the modern Olympic games.

FACT 5
The first woman to make a space flight (in 1963) was Valentina Tereshkova of the Soviet Union.

★ Work with others to plan and hold a panel discussion on the part women have played in the American space program.

★ Pretend you are attending a summer space camp for future astronauts. Write a letter home explaining what you do there.

FACT 6

The first woman to earn a medical degree was Elizabeth Blackwell.

⭐ Pretend you are Elizabeth Blackwell. Write and deliver a speech in which you tell not only about your struggle to become a doctor but also your later accomplishments.

⭐ Interview a woman doctor. Find out information such as why she decided to become a doctor and what training she needed. Also ask if she thinks there still is any discrimination against women in the medical field. Then report your findings.

FACT 7

The first woman astronomer was Maria Mitchell. In October 1847, a new comet, which she had sighted, was named after her.

⭐ Create a mobile that illustrates the path of Halley's Comet, the most famous comet. Include general information about comets.

⭐ Pretend you are an astronomer whose life work is the study of black holes. Write a letter to another astronomer in which you explain what you have learned about black holes and what mysteries still remain.

FACT 8

The first women to win a Nobel Prize for literature was Pearl S. Buck.

⭐ Create a collage that illustrates important events in her life. Then explain your collage to the class.

⭐ Read a book about China—such as The Good Earth by Pearl S. Buck—and write a book report about it.

FACT 9

The first woman to be elected to Congress was Jeannette Rankin. In 1916, the Republicans of MT elected her to the House of Representatives.

⭐ Create a timeline that shows the important developments that led to the current two-party system of Republicans and Democrats in the U.S. Include important information in labels and captions.

⭐ Pretend you are running for Congress: Plan your platform. Then hold a press conference in class in which you present your platform. Afterwards, members of the class could ask questions.

FACT 10

The founder and first president of the Girl Scouts was Juliette Gordon Low.

⭐ Write and illustrate a section in a children's encyclopedia that recounts the history of the Girl Scouts or the Boy Scouts.

⭐ If you are a Girl Scout or a Boy Scout, give a demonstration of some of the badges that scouts can earn and explain some of the activities that scouts participate in.

FOOD FACTS

FACT 1
Apples are 84% water.

★ Write a nutrition leaflet that explains the reasoning behind the old saying, "An apple a day keeps the doctor away."

★ Apples belong to the fruit group of foods. Create a poster that illustrates the government's recently published food pyramid, and include important information—such as the recommended daily helpings of each group.

FACT 2
Eighteen ounces of an average cola drink contain as much caffeine as a cup of coffee.

★ Write an article for your school newspaper in which you explore the addictive nature of caffeine and whether or not soft drinks do really quench thirst.

★ Write a segment for a TV program called "Your Health." The subject of the segment is water—how drinking it helps every part of the body.

FACT 3
Honey is the only food that does not spoil.

★ Pretend you are a queen bee. Write what you would say to instruct a group of young bees on making honey.

★ Work with others to hold a panel discussion on the pros and cons of artificial sweeteners like Equal®, and Sweet and Low®.

FACT 4
The average American eats 40 hotdogs a year. That is enough hotdogs each year to form a chain that would stretch from the earth to the moon and back again.

★ With a partner, write and act out a skit between a doctor and a patient in which the doctor tries to explain how harmful fat can be to the patient's health.

★ Make a poster called "Hints for Eating Smart."

FACT 5
In medieval England, beer was often served with breakfast.

★ Write a story, which is based on fact, about the effect alcohol can have on the body and the mind.

★ Peer pressure often leads young people to try alcohol. Write and act out a play showing how a young person might resist this pressure. Write to Alateen, Al-Anon Family Group, Headquarters, Inc., P.O. Box 182, Madison Square Station, New York, NY 10159.

FACT 6

Rice is the main food for half the people of the world.

⭐ Create a recipe for a rice dish that teenagers would like. Then explain how rice is grown and why it is so nutritional.

⭐ Write an editorial that compares the rate of hunger throughout the world. Then emphasize the problem of hunger in America, a land of such abundance. At the end, offer some possible solutions for this problem.

FACT 7

Ancient Greeks and Romans believed that crocodile blood would restore failing eyesight and that strawberry roots could cure mad-dog bites.

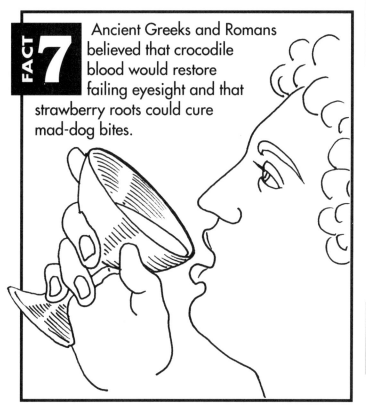

⭐ Create and illustrate a chart that shows the ideas people have about healthy foods today—from a medical point of view. For example, some think that carrots produce better eyesight. Then point out which ideas are true and which are not.

⭐ Plan a live demonstration that proves that foods that are healthy do not have to taste bad. Show ways to prepare healthy foods in new and tasty ways.

FACT 8

The pizza served to Queen Margharita of Italy was garnished with the colors of the Italian flag: white cheese, green basil, and red tomatoes.

⭐ Create a diagram that shows what is nutritionally good about pizza. However, also explain what is not so good about toppings like pepperoni and sausage.

⭐ Plan a live demonstration on how to make a pizza at home. As you prepare the pizza, explain how to use healthy ingredients.

FACT 9

If you want to cool off, do not eat ice cream. Although ice cream feels cool, it will actually make your body warmer because it is loaded with calories (units of heat).

⭐ Create a TV commercial for a yogurt company that explains why eating yogurt is healthier than eating ice cream.

⭐ Create a bulletin board about junk food. Define junk food, tell what is wrong with it, and offer substitutes for junk food.

FACT 10

In a lifetime, the average American who lives to be 70 years old will eat 880 chickens, 14 beef cattle, 23 hogs, 35 turkeys, 12 sheep, and 770 pounds of fish.

⭐ Write and illustrate a magazine article that explains what is wrong with eating a lot of red meat.

⭐ Work with other students to write a play about a teenager who has anorexia or bulimia. In addition to your own research, you may want to write to the American Anorexia/Bulimia Association, Inc., 133 Cedar Lane, Teaneck, NJ 07666.

GREAT COMPOSERS

FACT 1 Ludwig van Beethoven (1770-1827) started to lose his hearing when he was 32, and he was totally deaf when he wrote his Ninth Symphony.

★ Pretend you've seen a movie about Beethoven. Write a review of it that includes all the major plot points.

★ Give an oral report on the life of Johann Sebastian Bach (1685-1750), who continued to compose music after he was totally blind.

FACT 2 Wolfgang Amadeus Mozart (1756-1791), the greates musical genius the world has ever known, wrote 2 minuets at 5 years of age and a complete symphony at 8.

★ Pretend you are Mozart. In a series of diary entries, write about your life and your music.

★ Create a timeline about Felix Mendelssohn (1809-1847), who wrote his famous overture *A Midsummer's Night's Dream* when he was only 17.

FACT 3 In addition to writing symphonies, Johannes Brahms (1833-1897) wrote *Brahms' Lullaby*, also known as *Lullaby and Good Night*, the most famous lullaby ever.

★ Write and illustrate a short biography about Brahms.

★ Richard Wagner (1813-1883) was a great composer who was prejudiced. His music was favored by members of the Nazi Party. In an essay, give your opinion (based on facts) on whether a prejudiced person's art should be respected.

FACT 4 Giuseppe Verdi (1813-1901) wrote his famous opera *Aida* to commemorate the opening of the Suez Canal in 1871. For its premiere performance, Verdi even included live elephants in the production.

★ With a partner, plan and tape record an interview between a reporter and Verdi. Include information about his life and his most famous work.

★ Write and illustrate a magazine article about another composer of operas, Giacomo Puccini (1858-1924), who wrote *Madame Butterfly* and *La Boheme*.

FACT 5 Peter Ilich Tchaikovsky (1840-1893), the most popular 19th century Russian composer, wanted his *1812 Overture* to be played outdoors with the ringing of church bells, live cannon fire, and fireworks. It was performed that way for the first time in Moscow in 1990.

★ Write the script for a TV program called "This Is Your Life, Tchaikovsky."

★ Tape record an oral biography of Sergei Prokofiev (1891-1953), who wrote his first opera, *The Giant* at age 8 after seeing Tchaikovsky's *The Sleeping Beauty*.

FACT 6 The music of Frédéric Chopin (1810-1849) has become the most frequently played piano music in history.

⭐ Work with others to write a one-act play about the life of Chopin. Then rehearse it and present it to the class.

⭐ Create a timeline that highlights the major events in the life of Sergei Vassilievitch Rachmaninoff (1873-1943), who was a great composer as well as an extraordinary concert pianist.

FACT 7 Although he was French, Maurice Ravel (1875-1937) drew his inspiration from Spanish characteristics when he wrote *Boléro*.

⭐ After you tell the rest of the class about Ravel's life, play *Bolero* and have the students write what they see in their minds. Then share some of your impressions.

⭐ Create a storyboard about the life of Claude Debussy (1862-1918), who trained with Ravel in Paris.

FACT 8 Finland proclaimed a national holiday in honor of Jean Sibelius (1865-1957) on his 50th birthday.

⭐ Pretend you are Sibelius. Write a thank you letter to the people of Finland, telling them about your life and what inspired you to write *Finlandia*.

⭐ Write an announcement for an award for Edvard Grieg (1843-1907), another Scandinavian composer, for his famous work, *Peer Gynt*.

FACT 9 Igor Stravinsky (1882-1971) was the only living composer whose music was used in Walt Disney's movie *Fantasia*. Stravinsky's *The Rite of Spring* accompanies animated scenes of erupting volcanoes, prehistoric forests, and battling dinosaurs.

⭐ With a partner, write and tape record a conversation between Disney and Stravinsky, in which they discuss Stravinsky's life as well as his music.

⭐ Stavinsky's musical style has been compared to the artistic style of Pablo Picasso (1881-1973). Create a picture essay of Picasso and his work, which includes a 1920 portrait of Stravinsky.

FACT 10 George Gershwin (1898-1937), who was born in Brooklyn, NY, only started piano lessons at 13 but continued to take them for the next 35 years of his life.

⭐ Pretend you are Gershwin. In a series of diary entries, write about your life and your music.

⭐ Pretend you were a reporter for the New York Times when Leonard Bernstein (1918-1990), the composer/conductor, died. Write an article about his life and music.

INNER PLANETS

FACT 1 If a scaled-down version of the sun were placed on the goal line of a football field, Mercury, Venus, and Earth would all sit within the 20-yard line. Mars would be just inside the 30, and Jupiter would occupy the opposite goal line— 100 yards away. Saturn would be another football field away, Uranus 4 away, Neptune nearly 7, and Pluto 10 football fields away.

⭐ Make a mobile of the sun and the 9 planets. Scale it to reflect the actual distances between the planets.

⭐ Make and illustrate a chart that shows the major similarities and differences among the four inner planets.

FACT 2 In 1974, *Mariner 10* confirmed that Caloris Basin, the largest crater on Mercury, is bigger than Texas.

⭐ Work with others to plan and hold a panel discussion in which different members explain how craters, rays, and scarps were probably formed on Mercury.

⭐ Pretend you are a space-age detective. Discover the mystery of Vulcan: the appearing and disappearing neighboring planet to Mercury in the mid 19th century. Tape record your findings.

FACT 3 An entire year on Mercury lasts only 85 Earth days. As a result, if you are 10 years old on Earth, you would be age 41½ in Mercury years.

⭐ Write and rehearse a monologue about the Roman mythical god called Mercury. Include the reason why Mercury is a good name for the planet closest to the sun.

⭐ Give an oral report that covers what *Mariner 10* revealed about Mercury that scientists had not known before.

FACT 4 A day on Venus lasts 243 Earth days; a year lasts 225 Earth days. Therefore, Venus's day is longer than its year.

⭐ Write a newspaper article that explains what was learned about the surface of Venus after the *Pioneer-Venus I* mission in 1980.

⭐ Write a science fiction story that takes place before space probes were able to penetrate Venus's thick atmosphere. Base the story on actual facts about Venus.

FACT 5 The temperature on the surface of Venus is about 900 degrees F., making the surface of Venus hotter than the surface of any other planet in the solar system.

⭐ Pretend you are a third-grade science teacher. Write an explanation of Venus's hot surface that your students would understand. Include diagrams and pictures.

⭐ With a partner, discover how the earth is becoming more and more like Venus. For example, is there any evidence to suggest that Venus suffered from the greenhouse effect? Then tape record your findings.

 FACT 6
If the earth's orbit were 1% farther from the sun, all of its water would have frozen about 2 billion years ago.

★ Write a rap that explains some of the unique circumstances that contribute to the existence of life on Earth.

★ Pretend you are a Martian who has landed on the earth. In a series of journal entries, write about the things that surprise you the most.

 FACT 7
If you could take a walk on the moon tomorrow, you would see the footprints of Neil Armstrong, which were made during his July 20, 1969. That is because the moon is a dead, airless world.

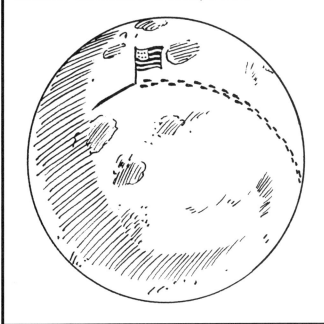

★ Write and illustrate a tour guide for future moon tourists. Include such helpful information as proper clothing, lodging facilities, and recreational activities.

★ Write a book report on Jules Verne's story "A Journey to the Moon" or another science fiction story about one of the inner planets or their moons.

 FACT 8
If you traveled from Earth to Mars in an existing spacecraft, your trip would take 7 months because you would have to cover 49 million miles.

★ Pretend you are one of the first astronauts to take a trip to Mars. As you orbit the planet, describe Olympus Mons, Mars' largest mountain (and explain how you know it is a volcano.)

★ Before astronauts can travel to Mars, scientists need to solve all the problems that result from long periods of weightlessness. Pretend you are a NASA scientist. Write a report on these problems.

 FACT 9
The average temperature on Mars is - 63 F, compared to the average temperature of 59 F on Earth.

★ With a partner, plan a debate about the following topic: Life might have existed on Mars at one time.

★ Pretend you are a NASA scientist. Write part of a training manual for astronauts that explains the reasons why spacesuits are a must during a Mars landing.

 FACT 10
If you weigh 100 pounds, a jump that would send you upward one foot on Earth would send you 1,000 feet upward on Phobos, one of Mars' two moons.

★ Pretend you are a science fiction writer, and you are working on a story about creatures from Phobos. Write an accurate description of your setting.

★ Draw a picture that shows what Mars would look like from Phobos. Then write an explanation of your picture.

INVENTORS

FACT 1

Thomas Edison, the inventor of the phonograph and electric lamp— among many other things—once said, "Invention is one percent inspiration and 99 percent perspiration."

⭐ Create a collage that includes some of Edison's 1,093 patented inventions. Include captions that explain each one of them.

⭐ Research the life of an inventor which seems to prove Edison's statement. Then write and illustrate a biography about that inventor.

FACT 2

Sixteen-year-old Alexander Graham Bell designed a rubber doll's head that said "Mama." What he learned from this early invention later helped him to invent the telephone.

⭐ With a partner, plan an interview between a reporter and an older Alexander Bell. The interview should cover the steps he had to take to invent the telephone and the reasons for his invention.

⭐ Work with others to find examples that prove that inventors can be any age. Then pretend one of you is the host of a TV show called "Inventors." Plan and video tape interviews between the host and each of the inventors.

FACT 3

Leonardo da Vinci, best known as an artist, was also a great inventor. Long before the world was ready for his inventions, da Vinci drew plans for a flying machine (airplane), horseless wagons (automobiles), and a parachute.

⭐ Create a bulletin board that features and describes some of da Vinci's modern inventions. Include important information in captions.

⭐ Like da Vinci, write your thoughts and ideas about the future in a series of journal entries. Also include plans and diagrams for at least a couple of futuristic inventions.

FACT 4

A dog contributed to the invention of Velcro®.

⭐ With a partner, find the story about the invention of Velcro®. Then, based on the story, write a skit and enact it for the class. In it include the various uses of Velcro® both in space and on the earth.

⭐ Research another invention that came about as a result of curiosity. Write about it as if it were a late-breaking TV news story.

FACT 5

When astronauts could not use ordinary ballpoint pens in space because they had no gravity to force the ink out, American Paul Fisher invented the Fisher Space Pen, which is now used not only in space but also throughout the world.

⭐ Create a board game based on the many products that were originally invented for space but are now used on the earth.

 Work with others to determine additional problems caused by lack of gravity in space. Then plan a show-and-tell that reports both the problems and the solutions the group came up with.

FACT 6 If James Marshall had not discovered gold on Captain Sutter's land in California in 1848, Levi jeans might never have been invented.

 Research and write the story of Levi Strauss and his invention of jeans. Then give a dramatic reading of your story to the class.

 Levi Strauss listened and responded to the needs of the people around him. With a partner, think about the needs for different kinds of clothing in the future. Then draw up plans and examples of clothing to meet those needs. Share your ideas with the class.

FACT 7 Some inventors have taken a common item already in existence and have found a new use for it. That is what Walter Fred Morrison did when he invented the Frisbee.

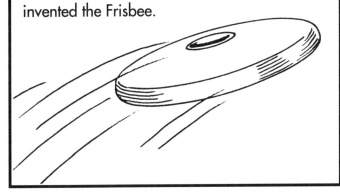

 With a partner, plan and write an interview between a reporter and Morrison after the Frisbee became popular.

 Work with others to think of some common objects—such as a comb, a fork, a hose, and a pillow—and some new uses for each of them. Then publish your inventions in a book with illustrations and explanations.

FACT 8 John Montagu—known also as the fourth Earl of Sandwich—invented the sandwich because he was a gambler and did not want to stop gambling to eat. Instead, when he got hungry, he gobbled some meat between two slices of bread.

 Prepare and deliver as an oral report: the story of John and Bill Kellogg and how they came to invent the first breakfast cereal.

 Invent a food for the future. It can be something brand new, or you can take an existing food and add a new twist to it. Then write a letter to your mother telling her about your invention.

FACT 9 Guglielmo Marconi used his brother's help in the early stages of his invention of the radio.

 Work with others to write a PBS radio program that tells the history of radio.

 Find out about other inventors who worked cooperatively with others—inventors like Whitcomb L. Judson, who invented the zipper. Tell about that inventor's life in a picture essay.

FACT 10 The movie *2001: A Space Odyssey* features a computer named HAL, which has a mind of its own. It decides, for example, to save the spaceship without consulting the astronauts.

 Write a newspaper article that predicts the capabilities that computers and/or robots will have in the future.

 Write an editorial for the school newspaper in which you argue for or against the need for every student to have the use of a computer in each classroom.

MAYA CIVILIZATION

FACT 1
During the Classic Period of Maya history, as many as 75,000 people lived in one city. (That is approximately the same number of people who presently live in Norwalk, Connecticut or Lake Charles, Louisiana.)

⭐ Make a timeline of the three periods of Maya history: Archaic Period, Pre-Classic Period, and Classic Period. Include drawings and captions that describe each period.

⭐ Plan a time capsule of things that represent each of the three stages. Label each one to explain its importance.

FACT 2
Stelas (stone slabs), which could be taller than 20 feet, were erected to honor the important events in the lives of Maya leaders.

⭐ Create and illustrate a children's book about one of the Maya leaders.

⭐ Create a bulletin board that explains the Maya class system that existed especially during the Classic Period.

FACT 3
The Maya calculated the length of a year as 365.2420 days. Today—over 1000 years later—the figure has been calculated at 365.2422 days.

⭐ Pretend you are a third grade teacher. Plan a lesson that explains Maya understanding and use of astronomy. Include visual aids for better understanding.

⭐ Create a storyboard that shows what happened at the Maya religious ceremony that took place every 52 years when the religious and regular Maya calendars came together.

FACT 4
The Maya were one of only three people in all of history to discover the zero. As a result, they were able to count in very large numbers.

⭐ Give a demonstration of how the Maya mathematical system worked.

⭐ Imagine that you could go back in time and interview a Maya priest about the different ways the Maya people used math in their lives. With a partner, plan and write out the interview. Then present the interview to the class.

FACT 5
David Stuart, an American 8-year-old, was one of the first people to understand the written language of the Maya.

⭐ Pretend you are David Stuart. In a series of journal entries, explain how you figured out what the various glyphs (drawings used in Maya writing) meant.

⭐ Pretend you are an archaeologist. Hold a press conference in which you explain the new information you learned about the Maya once you and other archaeologists understood the written Maya language.

Maya not only carved messages into stone, but they also recorded a lot of information in books.

⭐ Write a magazine article that describes the Maya book called the Dresen Codex. Then explain why so few of the Maya books remain today.

⭐ Create a facsimile of a Maya book. In it, include examples of the Maya glyphs and their meanings.

Itzamná, which was often pictured as a lizard-like creature with two heads, was probably the most important Maya god at the time of the Spanish conquest.

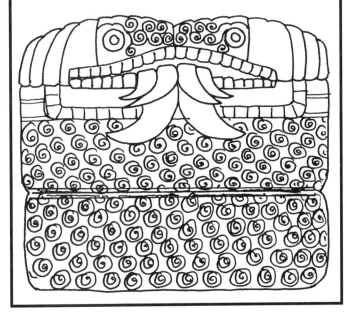

⭐ Create a picture essay that tells about some of the Maya gods and their powers.

⭐ Write and illustrate a section in a children's history book that explains the role religion had in the everyday lives of the Maya during the Classic Period.

Starting with Hernando Cortes, Spanish conquistadors—under the banner "God, Glory, and Gold"—almost succeeded in wiping out the Maya culture.

⭐ Work with others to write, rehearse, and present a one-act play in which Cortes and his soldiers recount their victories over the Maya. Include the reasons why they were so victorious.

⭐ Give an oral report that gives a modern example of one group of people trying to destroy another people and their culture.

Between about 800 to 900 A.D., nearly all Maya in the southern lowlands abandoned their cities.

⭐ Work with others to plan and hold a panel discussion that covers the different theories that have been proposed to explain this strange event.

⭐ Pretend you are a South American tour guide. Write a speech that you would give tourists to explain why it took almost 1,000 years before Maya ruins were found.

Most of the more than 6 million modern Maya live in rural areas of Mexico, Guatemala, and Belize.

⭐ Plan an educational TV show that explains what happened to many of the Maya who were living in Guatemala, during the 1970s.

⭐ Write and illustrate a magazine article about the life of modern Maya.

NATIONAL PARKS

FACT 1
The states of Rhode Island and Delaware would fit inside Yellowstone National Park and still have room to spare—making Yellowstone the biggest, as well as the oldest, national park.

⭐ Prepare a tourist guide to Yellowstone National Park—with pictures and maps.

⭐ Write a letter back home to a friend—telling all about the more than 200 geysers at Yellowstone National Park.

FACT 2
The British, who controlled Florida from 1763 - 1783 after taking it from Spain in a war, named a large section of swampland Everglades because the area at that time resembled an everlasting "glade," or open meadow.

⭐ Create a bulletin board that highlights some of the unique wildlife that lives in the Everglades National Park.

⭐ Write and illustrate a mini dictionary that features the various endangered species that presently live in the Everglades National Park.

FACT 3
At the Glacier National Park in MT, you can still see over 50 glaciers.

⭐ Draw a map of the Glacier National Park and show how you would cross the Continental Divide at 6,664 feet if you followed the Going-to-the Sun Road at the Glacier National Park.

⭐ Create a mobile that describes wildlife at the Glacier National Park.

FACT 4
Some of the sequoia trees, which have been growing at Yosemite National Park in CA for nearly 3,000 years, have bark two feet thick and branches bigger around than the trunks of most full-grown oak trees.

⭐ Give an oral report on the unusual sequoia trees. Be sure to include pictures, graphs, and other visual aides.

⭐ Write a tall tale that explains how the sequoia trees became so huge.

FACT 5
There are more than 300 miles of underground passages in the Mammoth Cave National Park in KY.

⭐ Work with others to plan and hold a panel discussion that explains some of the unusual formations, fish, and animals in the caves.

⭐ With a partner, plan, write, and video tape an interview between a reporter and a park ranger. During the interview discuss the duties and problems of a ranger.

FACT 6

Crater Lake, which is 6 miles across, is in Crater Lake National Park in Oregon. At 1,932 feet deep, it is the deepest lake in the U.S.

⭐ Find the legend the Klamath Indians told—about 6,800 years ago—to explain the formation of Crater Lake. Then give an oral reading of the legend to the class.

⭐ Create a storyboard with captions that explains how Crater Lake was formed.

FACT 7

The oldest rock layers in the Grand Canyon in Arizona date back 2 million years.

⭐ Pretend you are a tour guide for a trip down the rapids of the Colorado River through the Grand Canyon. Write and tape what you would explain along the way.

⭐ Pretend you are Major John W. Powell. In diary entries, explain how you were able to map the Grand Canyon in 1869.

FACT 8

In 1901, Guglielmo Marconi built four tall wooden towers on the shores of Cape Cod in MA. He used these towers to send his first telegraphic messages across the Atlantic Ocean.

⭐ Write and illustrate a booklet about the history of the Cape Cod National Seashore—including how it got its name.

⭐ Work with others to write, rehearse, and present a one-act play about the time Captain Miles Standish stopped the Mayflower at Cape Cod before landing permanently at Plymouth.

FACT 9

Three million years ago, scientists say, huge glaciers—some half-a-mile thick—moved through Yosemite Valley, creating the deep gorges, the sheer cliffs, the jagged peaks, and the rounded domes.

⭐ Pretend you are President Theodore Roosevelt. Write the speech he might have begun when he said, "Yosemite is the most beautiful place on Earth."

⭐ Write and illustrate a guide to safe rock climbing, which forest rangers could hand out to tourists.

FACT 10

At the Great Smokey Mountain National Park in NC and TN, 16 mountain peaks soar more than a mile high.

⭐ Create a time capsule of tagged articles that explains what life must have been like for the first pioneers who lived 200 years ago in what is now the Great Smokey Mountain National Park.

⭐ Write a newspaper article for the travel section of your local newspaper that describes the outdoor museum in the Great Smokey Mountain National Park.

OUTER PLANETS

FACT 1

The "red spot" on Jupiter is so large that three Earths could fit inside it.

⭐ Pretend you are an astronaut flying past Jupiter. In your official report, describe the red spot and explain what it is.

⭐ Write a NASA report to Congress that tells what scientists learned about Jupiter from the *Pioneer* and *Voyager* missions and what they still hope to learn from the *Galileo* mission when it arrives there in 1995.

FACT 2

Io, one of Jupiter's moons, is the most volcanically active body in the solar system. Its volcanoes spurt liquid sulfur and sulfur dioxide at speeds of up to 2,340 mph.

⭐ Write an article for *Space* magazine that explains how Galileo used Jupiter's moons to prove that the earth was not the center of the universe.

⭐ Create a bulletin board that highlights Jupiter's four moons. Explain the possibility of life on Europa.

FACT 3

From outside edge to opposite outside edge, the rings of Saturn stretch almost 600,000 miles.

⭐ Pretend you are a space detective. Report on the origin of the rings.

⭐ Create a poster that explains what keeps the rings in place.

FACT 4

Saturn has more moons than any other planet—at least 20.

⭐ Create a mobile that highlights the differences among Saturn's moons.

⭐ Pretend you are a spokesperson for NASA. Write and video tape the response you would give to a reporter's question about the possibility that life might exist on Titan, one of Saturn's moons. In your response, include some facts about Titan and explain what makes it so unusual.

FACT 5

Because Uranus is 1½ billion miles from the sun—19 times Earth's distance from the sun—it takes the planet 84 Earth years to get around the sun.

⭐ Draw a diagram that explains why one of Uranus's poles receives 42 years of daylight while the other has a 42-year night as the planet travels around the sun.

⭐ Write a NASA leaflet that explains how Uranus was discovered.

FACT 6

Miranda, one of the oldest moons in the entire solar system, is one of the 15 moons that orbit Uranus.

⭐ Pretend you are an astronomer. Write a letter to another astronomer in which you explain why Miranda's land surface was such a surprise after the Voyager II mission and why it is still an unsolved mystery.

⭐ Work with a partner to write and tape record an interview between a reporter and a NASA scientist. During the interview explain why Uranus's rings were a surprise and how they were discovered even before the *Voyager II* mission.

FACT 7

Pluto, although called a planet, may actually be an asteroid of the outer solar system.

⭐ Pretend you are on a quiz show and are asked the following question: Why is the following statement both true and false: Pluto is the planet farthest from the sun? Write your answer.

⭐ Write and illustrate a section for a science book that explains the discovery of Pluto.

FACT 8

If you exposed your bare hand while visiting Uranus, Neptune, or Pluto, it would be freeze-dried instantly because temperatures around these planets stay colder than -350 F.

⭐ Write a fictitious tour of Uranus and Neptune and explain why they might contain many diamonds.

⭐ Pretend you are a space detective. Write a report that explains why some scientists think there is a 10th planet beyond Pluto.

FACT 9

A spacecraft called *Pioneer 10*, launched by the U.S. in 1972, has now passed beyond Pluto's orbit.

⭐ Write a newspaper article that explains what scientists learned from the *Pioneer 10* mission that they had not known before.

⭐ Research the following message attached to *Pioneer 10* that was carried beyond our solar system. Tell what it means to you. Then create your own message.

FACT 10

The Hubble Space Telescope, which was launched in 1990, promised to find out more about Jupiter and Saturn.

⭐ Write and video tape a TV news report about the launch of the Hubble and what was learned shortly after it was in orbit.

⭐ Write a NASA report to Congress that explains what is wrong with the Hubble Space Telescope and what can be done to correct it.

FACT 1

Matthew Henson (1866-1955) was the first person to reach the North Pole—even though Robert E. Peary is usually given the credit.

⭐ Create a picture essay of Henson's life. Include important information in captions.

⭐ Write a biography of a modern black explorer such as Guion Stewart Bluford, Jr., an astronaut on the Challenger shuttle, or Dr. May C. Jemison, an astronaut on the Endeavour shuttle.

FACT 2

In 1947, Jackie Robinson (1919-1972) became the first black player to play in baseball's major leagues.

⭐ Write a script for a TV show called This Is Your Life, Jackie Robinson.

⭐ Give an oral report on the life of another famous black athlete such as Reggie Jackson, Earvin "Magic" Johnson, or Leroy "Satchel" Paige.

FACT 3

In 1939, Marian Anderson (1902-1993), a famous opera singer, was barred from singing in Constitution Hall in Washington D.C. because she was black.

⭐ Pretend you are Eleanor Roosevelt, the wife of the President. In a letter to the newspaper, tell about Anderson's life and the reason why you resigned from the DAR to protest her not being allowed to sing.

⭐ Work with others to write and act out a short play about the life of another famous black musician such as "Duke" Ellington, Louis Armstrong, or Scott Joplin.

FACT 4

At 26 years of age, Lorraine Hansberry (1930-1965) became the first black woman to have a play produced on Broadway.

⭐ Pretend you were a reporter for the New York Times when Hansberry died in 1965. Write an article that tells about her life and her accomplishments.

⭐ Write a biography of another black playwright such as James Baldwin.

FACT 5

As a result of his invention of a small refrigerator unit, Frederick McKinley Jones (1893-1961) changed the eating habits of everyone in the world.

⭐ Write what would have been said at a press conference to announce Jones's new invention. At the same time, tell about the inventor himself.

⭐ Create a comic strip that tells the life of another black inventor such as Garrett A. Morgan, who invented the gas mask.

FACT 6

After Harriet Tubman (1821-1913) escaped from slavery in 1849, she was wanted "Dead or Alive" with a $40,000 reward offered for her capture.

 Pretend you are Harriet Tubman. Write diary entries that tell about your experiences as a slave and what you did once you escaped.

Write a children's biography of another famous abolitionist, Frederick Douglass.

FACT 7

After Martin Luther King, Jr., was shot, 100,000 people gathered outside the church where his funeral was held.

Create a picture essay of the life of King. Include important information in captions.

Give an oral report on another black activist such as Jesse Jackson, Roy Wilkins, or Rosa Parks.

FACT 8

Thurgood Marshall (1908-1993) became the first black man to be appointed to the U.S. Supreme Court in 1967.

 Create a timeline of his life, including the important civil rights cases he won as the Chief Counsel for the NAACP.

Write an entry in the Who's Who in U.S. Government about another black public servant such as Colin Powell, the head of the Joint Chiefs of Staff.

FACT 9

During his career as a track and field athlete, Jesse Owens (1913-1980) broke 7 world records and handed Adolf Hitler a crushing defeat in the 1936 Olympics in Germany.

Write a poem or a rap song that tells about Owens's life and accomplishments.

Write a newspaper article that covers the life and accomplishments of another black Olympic winner such as Wilma Rudolph or Carl Lewis.

FACT 10

One recent triumph of Maya Angelou (1928-) was reading a poem of hers at President Clinton's Inauguration in 1993.

With a partner, plan and tape record an interview between a reporter and Angelou. Discuss her life and her writing.

Write a children's biography of another famous black writer such as Langston Hughes, Arna Bontemps, Alice Walker, or Toni Morrison.

OUTSTANDING HISPANIC AMERICANS

FACT 1
Chosen from 2,000 applicants, Dr. Ellen Ochoa (1959-) became the first Hispanic female astronaut.

⭐ Write a script for a TV show called "This Is Your Life, Ellen Ochoa."

⭐ With a partner, write and tape record an interview with another Hispanic adventurer such as Everett Alvarez, Jr., a Navy pilot, or Manuel Lisa, a trader and explorer.

FACT 2
Critics all agreed that the exotic beauty and brilliant technique of Evelyn Cisneros (1958-) made her an outstanding prima ballerina.

⭐ Write and illustrate a children's biography about the life and accomplishments of Cisneros.

⭐ Create a comic strip about another Hispanic dancer such as José Limon.

FACT 3
After earning a Ph.D. in English from the University of California, Richard Rodriquez (1948-) wrote his autobiography called *Hunger of Memory*.

⭐ In a story-like fashion, tell the class about Rodriquez's life.

⭐ Create a bulletin board about the lives of other Hispanic writers like Oscar Hijuelos and Luis Valdes.

FACT 4
The first time he ran for mayor of San Antonio, TX, Henry Cisneros (1947-) got 62% of the vote. Running for a second term, he got almost 95% of the vote. In 1993, he became the Secretary of Housing and Urban Development in President Clinton's cabinet.

⭐ Write an encyclopedia entry about the life and accomplishments of Cisneros.

⭐ Write a magazine article about another Hispanic governmental official such as Antonia Novello, a U.S. Surgeon General, or Dennis Chávez, the first Hispanic senator.

FACT 5
"From my earliest days," Pablo Casals (1876-1973) once told a friend, "music was for me...an activity as normal as breathing." Casals became a world famous cellist, composer, and conductor.

⭐ Tape record some of Casals' music and as you play it, tell about the major events in his life.

⭐ Give an oral report on the life of another famous Hispanic creative artist, Louis Agassíz Fuertes.

FACT 6 According to Rolling Stone magazine, Linda Ronstadt (1946-) owes her success to "her good looks, her charm, her ear for harmony, but above all to her voice, which is about the most versatile and strong and most alluring vocal sound in pop music."

⭐ Add to this article in Rolling Stone magazine by telling about Ronstadt's life and accomplishments.

⭐ Write a biographical sketch about another famous Hispanic singer such as Ritchie Valens or Joan Baez.

FACT 7 When he was born, the parents of César Chávez (1927-1993) were farm owners, but they eventually lost their farm and had to become migrant farm workers. When he grew up, Chávez founded the United Farm Workers to improve conditions for migrant workers.

⭐ Write a poem or a rap song about Chávez's life.

⭐ Write a summary of a TV show for PBS about a Hispanic explorer in another generation such as Juan Ponce de León or Hernando De Soto.

FACT 8 The same year that Roberto Clemente (1934-1972) made his 300th hit, he died in a plane crash on his way to Nicaragua with relief supplies to earthquake victims.

⭐ Work with others to write and act out a short play about Clemente's life.

⭐ Write and illustrate a biography of the life of another Hispanic athlete such as Richard "Pancho" Gonzales, the tennis champion, or Michael Carbajal, the boxer.

FACT 9 Rita Moreno (1931-) began taking dancing lessons at the age of 5, and 20 years later, she played Anita in the film version of West Side Story.

⭐ Pretend you are a reporter for a magazine called Famous Hispanics. Write an article that tells about Moreno's life and accomplishments.

⭐ Create a poster about the life of another Hispanic actor such as Martin Sheen or Desi Arnaz.

FACT 10 While he was at the MIT Radiation Laboratory, Luis Alvarez, a Nobel Prize physicist, developed a radar beam so narrow that it could guide an airplane lost in fog to the ground.

⭐ Create a film strip about Alvarez's life. Then record a narration to go with it.

⭐ Give an oral report on the life of another famous Hispanic scientist such as Juan Guiteras, a medical researcher.

PLANET EARTH

FACT 1

Carbon dioxide, which is essential to plant life, makes up less than .04% of the earth's air.

☆ Create a graph that shows the percentages of different gases in the air. Then explain their uses to the class.

☆ Write a newspaper article that explains the connection between the .04% of carbon dioxide in the air and the rainforests in South America.

FACT 2

The equator is exactly 24,901.5 miles long.

☆ After you draw a map of the earth that includes the equator and all other imaginary lines, hold a class quiz. Give various sets of longitudes and latitudes and ask classmates to use them to find specific places on your map.

☆ Since lines like the equator are imaginary, they cannot be seen from space; however, many other things about the surface of the earth can be seen from space. Make a collage that includes many important pieces of information about the earth that astronauts and satellites have discovered. Label your collage.

FACT 3

The Pacific Ocean is larger than all the land in the world.

☆ Pretend you are the narrator for an episode of a radio program call "Sea World." Write and tape record an explanation of why the oceans are salty.

☆ Write to the America Oceans Campaign, 725 Arizona Avenue, Suite 102, Santa Monica, CA 90401, and request information about the oceans. Then report those findings along with your own research to the class.

FACT 4

Glaciers occupy 5.8 million square miles, or 10% of the land's surface. That is an area as large as South America.

☆ Create a picture essay that first explains what a glacier is and then shows how glaciers are responsible for much of the geography of the earth today.

☆ Contact your state geological office and find out if there is any evidence of glaciation in your local landscape. If there is, report your findings to the rest of the class.

FACT 5

The highest waves ever recorded on the earth were 1,740 feet high. That is higher than the Sears Tower in Chicago, which is the world's tallest building.

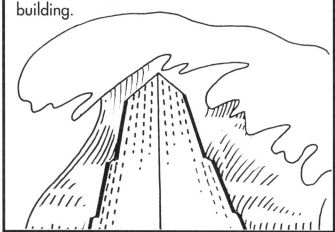

☆ Plan a demonstration that shows how waves are formed. (You may have to get some help from your science teacher.)

★ Create a bulletin board that gives a definition of tsunamis as well as some specific examples of their force and power.

FACT 6 The center of the earth may be hotter than the surface of the sun.

★ Give a demonstration that shows how the three layers of the earth can be compared to a soft boiled egg.

★ Pretend you are a detective. Investigate Project Mohole, a project to drill through the earth's crust into the mantle. Publish your findings in a report.

FACT 7 The moon moves about 2 inches farther away from the earth every year.

★ Draw a diagram that explains the relationship of the moon to the tides on the earth. Then explain it to the class.

★ Draw a chart that shows the different phases of the moon. Add captions and labels to explain each phase.

FACT 8 The only rocks in the ice of Antarctica are meteorites.

★ With a partner, plan an interview between a reporter and an astronomer, in which you discuss meteorites: what they are, why more do not hit the earth, and what would happen if a huge one did hit the earth.

★ Give an oral report that explains how scientists are learning about the earth's interior by studying meteorites. Also give examples of some of the meteorites that scientists have been able to study.

FACT 9 The Marianas Trench, in the Pacific Ocean, is 6.8 miles deep. If Mt. Everest were placed in the trench, its top would still be below the ocean's surface.

★ Because the ocean floor is the last undiscovered frontier on earth, find out what efforts are being made to explore the ocean's floor. Then use this factual information in a science fiction story with a surprise ending.

★ Work with others to plan and video tape a panel discussion on the present and possible future uses of the ocean as a source of mineral resources, fresh water, and a place for farming and ranching.

FACT 10 The earth once had a 435-day year.

★ Give an oral report that explains how a year on the earth is determined. Then offer a reasonable explanation for the fact that a year on the earth was once almost 100 days longer than it is today.

★ Investigate an early method of keeping track of time—such as Stonehenge in England, which was built over 3,000 years ago. Then, using pictures from a book, report your findings to the class.

PRESIDENTS

FACT 1 Thomas Jefferson could be considered a one-man "Yellow Pages" because he was all of the following: anthropologist, architect, bibliophile, botanist, classicist, diplomat, educator, ethnologist, farmer, geographer, gourmet, horseman, horticulturist, inventor, lawyer, lexicographer, linguist, mathematician, meteorologist, naturalist, numismatist, paleontologist, philosopher, politician, statesman, violinist, and writer.

★ Work with others to plan and hold a panel discussion in which the various members choose one or more of the professions listed above and explain how they applied to Jefferson.

★ Draw a series of pictures that illustrates the various professions listed above. Then quiz the rest of the class about which pictures match which professions.

FACT 2 The shortest inauguration speech, only 133 words, was delivered by George Washington at his second inaugural on March 4, 1793. His speech lasted two minutes.

★ Read aloud a famous inaugural address—such as John F. Kennedy's. Then explain what you think are the important points made in the speech.

★ Pretend you have just been elected President. Write your inaugural address, emphasing what you think are the most important issues needing attention.

FACT 3 Abraham Lincoln was the tallest President at 6 feet, 4 inches.

★ Make a silhouette of Lincoln, matching his height of 6'4". Then on the silhouette, draw a timeline —from foot to head—that includes all the major events in his life.

★ Give an oral report on the background and history of the Lincoln Monument, in which a sculpture shows Lincoln's tall body sitting in a huge chair.

FACT 4 During World War I, President Woodrow Wilson released the White House groundskeeper to join the Army. Then the President replaced him with sheep that kept the White House lawn nice and trim.

★ Pretend you are a United States soldier during World War I. Write some of your thoughts and ideas about the war in a series of journal entries.

★ Create a timeline that includes the major events that led up to World War I and the United States' involvement in that war.

FACT 5 The first President to live in the White House was John Adams, who moved in on November 1, 1800.

⭐ Pretend you are Abigail Adams. Write a letter to a friend in which you explain how White House life was at the beginning.

⭐ Write the history of the White House for a guide book that will be handed out to all White House visitors in the future.

 FACT 6 As boys, Presidents Millard Fillmore and Andrew Johnson were both indentured servants.

⭐ Give an oral report on how the indenture system worked back in the 1800s.

⭐ Pretend you are Millard Fillmore during the time he was indentured. As Fillmore, write a letter to a friend, stating what your life is like and what your hopes and dreams are.

 FACT 7 Abigail Adams was ahead of her time. In 1774, for example, she wrote to her husband John warning him that women would rebel if they were not given any representation in the new government.

⭐ Write and illustrate a children's biography of Abigail Adams.

⭐ Find some of Abigail Adams's letters to her husband. Then choose one to read aloud dramatically and discuss it with the class.

 FACT 8 President Andrew Jackson's nickname was Old Hickory because people said that he was as tough and hard as hictory wood.

⭐ Make a chart with the Presidents' names, their nicknames, and the reasons for their nicknames.

⭐ Work with others to explore the lives and accomplishments of these Presidents: John Adams, Thomas Jefferson, Ulysses S. Grant, Franklin Roosevelt, and Richard Nixon. Then come up with nicknames for each of them.

 FACT 9 Woodrow Wilson won the Nobel Peace Prize in 1919 for his efforts in creating the League of Nations after World War I.

⭐ Create a storyboard that shows the history of the League of Nations and what that organization eventually led to.

⭐ Write the words to a song or a poem that explains how World War I finally ended.

FACT 10 The faces of 4 Presidents are carved into Mt. Rushmore in South Dakota. The pupils of the eyes on the Presidents' faces are 4 feet across and their mouths are 18 feet wide.

⭐ With a partner, prepare an interview between a television reporter and Gutzon Borglum, the sculptor of Mt. Rushmore. Include Borglum's reasons for choosing to honor the four Presidents that he did.

⭐ Write and illustrate a tour guide to Mt. Rushmore, giving its history, the actual physical features of the monument, and facts about its upkeep.

PYRAMIDS

FACT 1 The Giza Pyramids, which were built nearly 5000 years ago in Egypt, are 480 feet tall. That means that they are almost 200 feet taller than the Statue of Liberty.

 Pretend you are visiting the Giza Pyramids. Write a letter home to your parents in which you draw a diagram of the pyramids and label and describe all the different places you explored.

 The Giza Pyramids are one of the Seven Wonders of the Ancient World. Write a section in an almanac that briefly describes each one of these wonders.

FACT 2 The Sphinx that guards the pyramids of Giza was originally painted with red and yellow—and perhaps with even other colors.

 Pretend you are a tour guide at the Giza Pyramids. Write the speech you would give tourists to explain what the Sphinx is and why it is there.

 Pretend you are the Sphinx. Tell about what you saw on the day that Pharaoh Khafre was buried.

FACT 3 The first pyramid was built out of stone around 2700 B.C.

 Make a timeline that includes the important events in the evolution of pyramids, starting in the earliest times, going up through the great pyramid at Giza, and ending at the Valley of the Kings.

 Work with others to plan and hold a panel discussion on the different theories people hold today that explain the construction of the pyramids. For example, how could pyramids, some of which cover an area greater than that of 10 football fields, be built without the use of any modern equipment like cranes and bulldozers?

FACT 4 In 1954, archaeologists found a sealed boat pit near the Great Pyramid.

 Pretend you are one of the 1954 archaeologists. Write a report that explains what you found in the pit and what you later learned about your discovery.

 Pretend you are an expert on Egyptian history. Prepare a speech in which you explain why pharaohs were buried with boats and so many other possessions.

FACT 5 The average weight of one of a pyramid's stone blocks is 2½ tons. That is the weight of two medium-sized cars. Some blocks, however, weighed up to 15 tons, the approximate weight of five elephants.

Give an oral report that explains the several reasons why Egypt was the natural place for pyramids to be built.

 Pretend you are a modern architect. Write a magazine article exploring whether pyramids could be built today, and, if they could, ways in which they could be used.

FACT 6 The third coffin of Pharaoh Tutankhamen, known as King Tut, was made out of 2,500 pounds of gold.

 Work with others to write and act out a skit in which some of the workers are discussing things such as what tools and methods they are using to build the pyramids and how they were recruited.

 Create a picture essay that describes the different chambers within a pyramid like the Great Pyramid at Giza.

FACT 7 Sometimes up to 100,000 men worked for 20 seasons on one pyramid.

 Write and illustrate a children's biography of King Tut.

 Pretend you are Howard Carter who found the sealed entrance to Tut's tomb in 1922. In a series of journal entries, write about your great discovery.

FACT 8 In about 1895 B.C., Sesostris II had a town built on the edge of the desert to house the men who were building his pyramid.

 Draw a picture of what that town might have looked like. Include captions that explain the different places and features of the town.

 Pretend you are a leading Egyptian historian. Write a chapter in a new book of yours that explains what happened to Sesostris's town and what historians like you have learned about the Egyptians from it.

FACT 9 As many as 410 yards of linen could be used to wrap a mummy. That is about as much material as it would take to go from the top to the bottom of the Empire State Building.

 Write and illustrate a chapter in a children's science book that explains the process of mummification. Include the reason the Egyptians used this method.

 Pretend you are a museum guide. Write a speech for groups of visitors that explains what modern people have learned about ancient Egyptians by the mummies that have been found and examined.

FACT 10 Today, Egyptologists believe that only 40% of Egypt's buried ruins have been found.

 Write and illustrate an article for the fictitious magazine *Ecology Today*. Stress how air pollution is currently affecting the pyramids.

 Work with others to research two modern pyramids: the pyramid at the Louvre in Paris and the Great American Pyramid in Memphis, TN. Then present your findings—along with pictures—to the class.

RAINFORESTS

FACT 1

Even though rainforests cover only 6% of the earth, they are home to more than one half of all living species on this planet.

⭐ Create a mobile that highlights and describes some of the familiar inhabitants of rainforests such as chimpanzees and jaguars.

⭐ Write a rap song that tries to convince people to stop the destruction of the rainforests.

FACT 2

It takes only a few minutes for a chain saw to topple a 7-foot-wide tree, but it would take 5 centuries for another tree to grow to the same size.

⭐ Give an oral report on the gathering of world leaders in Brazil in June 1992 to work out ways to stop the destruction of the rainforests. (Find information in newspaper and magazine articles.)

⭐ Create a bulletin board that stresses the need to preserve the rainforests.

FACT 3

Rainforests are the lungs of the earth.

⭐ Draw a poster that illustrates Fact 3. Then explain your poster to the class.

⭐ Create a storyboard for a public service announcement on TV that explains how the loss of trees in the rainforests has an effect on the rest of the world.

FACT 4

One quarter of all prescription drugs used in the U.S. originally came from tropical forest plants.

⭐ Work with others to plan and hold a panel discussion on current drugs that come from rainforest plants. For example, you could report on how the leaves of the rosy periwinkle plant are used to treat certain forms of cancer.

⭐ Draw a map of the area where most of the rainforests exist. Then mark the places where the forests have already been leveled, eliminating any healing drugs ever to come from those sections.

FACT 5

At least 27 million acres of rainforest are cut and burned every year. That means that each year an area about the size of Illinois is lost.

⭐ With a partner, prepare a debate between an American environmentalist and a poor South American farmer or a rancher who is burning down some of the trees in the rainforest in order to make a living.

Pretend you are an environmentalist. With a group, hold a press conference in which you explain the greenhouse effect.

FACT 6
M&M's don't melt in your hand because they are coated with a harmless wax that comes from tropical rainforests.

Give a show-and-tell presentation in which you include common everyday items that come—at least in part—from rainforests.

Make a collage showing all of the many benefits of the rainforests. Then explain it to the class.

FACT 7
Rainforests have a yearly rainfall of 75-325 inches—compared to 16 inches annually in Spokane, WA.

Draw a relief map that shows and explains the three layers of a typical rainforest.

Pretend you are a South American TV weather forecaster. Explorers watch your show. Write your prediction of the weather in the rainforest for the next week and rehearse it with a map of the area. Then video tape it.

FACT 8
One square mile of South America's Amazon rainforest may be home to as many as 1,500 species of butterflies. (There are only 750 species of butterflies in all of the U.S. and Canada.)

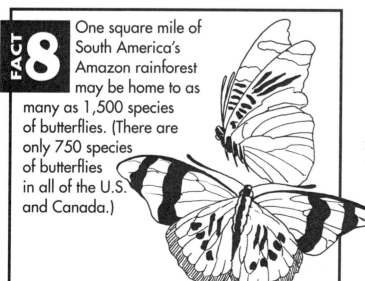

Draw the life cycle of a butterfly. Include all important information in labels and captions.

Research some of the unusual varieties of butterflies, draw their pictures, and then report on them to the rest of the class.

FACT 9
Some rodents in the rainforests weight as much as 100 pounds, and some daisies and violets there can be as big as an apple tree in the U.S.

Pretend you are a dictionary writer. First come up with a good definition of the word "camouflage". Then give a few examples of how some rainforest animals use camouflage to protect themselves.

Present a show-and-tell of an unusual animal, plant, or insect that presently lives in a rainforest.

FACT 10
Ben and Jerry's ice cream company supports the rainforests by buying hundreds of thousands of dollars worth of Brazilian nuts and cashews every year.

As a class, plan a school-wide "Save the Rainforests" campaign. For example, you could plan speeches, make posters and flyers, and write letters to local and state government officials.

Write to the Rainforest Alliance at 295 Madison Ave., Suite 1804, New York, New York 10017, and ask for information about rainforests. Then report your findings—along with your own research—to the class.

RECYCLING

FACT 1

New York City's nearly 8 million residents throw out enough garbage every month to fill up the entire Empire State Building.

 Find out how the garbage in your area is eliminated and if there are any plans for the future when that source runs out. Then in a series of cartoons, first show all of the different ways that garbage can be disposed of and highlight how your area disposes of its garbage.

 Plan a recycling program at your school. For some ideas, you can write to Kids Against Pollution, Tenahill School, 275 High St., Closter, NJ 07624.

FACT 2

In one month, Americans throw away enough beverage cans to reach the moon.

 Write and video tape a TV editorial about the need to recycle aluminum. Include all the aluminum products that can be recycled and specifically point out how energy is saved by recycling aluminum.

 As a class, plan a school wide fund-raising program by collecting cans. For ideas, you can write to Aluminum Assoc., 900 19th St. N.W., Washington, D.C. 20006.

FACT 3

The energy saved from recycling one glass bottle will light a 100-watt light bulb for 4 hours.

 Create a film strip that shows how glass is recycled. At the end, include ways to encourage people to recycle glass. Then record a narration for it.

 With a partner, plan a show-and-tell of the many creative ways to reuse glass jars—rather than throwing them out or even recycling them.

FACT 4

Americans throw away 2.5 million plastic bottles every hour, and only a very small percentage is recycled.

 Create a mobile that shows the many different products that plastic can be recycled into. Include an explanation of why plastic does not decompose in a landfill.

 Create a recycling board game. The goal should be to get people to recycle more.

FACT 5

It takes an entire forest—over 500,000 trees—to supply Americans with their Sunday newspapers every week.

 Find out how much newspaper is recycled in your town and find out what happens to the newspaper that is not recycled. Then explore what action is needed to increase the amount recycled. Include your findings in an article for your school newspaper.

 With a partner, find out all the products that newspaper can be recycled into. For help, you can write for a catalog from the Earth Care Paper Co., P.O. Box 3335, Madison WI 53704. Report your findings to the class.

FACT 6

About 100 million trees are used every year to produce almost 2 million tons of junk mail.

 How much junk mail does your family get in one week? With your parents' permission, stop most of the junk mail by writing to Mail Preference Service, Direct Marketing Assoc., 11 West 42nd St., P.O. Box 3861, NY, NY 10163.

 With a partner, come up with a list of suggestions for creative uses for your school's junk mail, used milk cartons, and other used and unused paper products. Then present your suggestions to the principal.

FACT 7

If you lined up all the styrofoam cups made in just one day, they would circle the earth at the equator.

 Write and video tape a TV press conference explaining the hazards of styrofoam to the earth and to sealife.

 Work with others to write a letter to the mayor of your town. Explain the problems with styrofoam and ask how much styrofoam is bought with government money. Then organize a campaign of posters and letters to get people—especially in government—to stop using styrofoam.

FACT 8

American use 2 million disposable batteries every year.

 Write and tape record a public service announcement that explains why batteries become hazardous if they are thrown into the garbage. Also include suggestions for disposing of them properly.

 Write to the Environmental Defense Fund, 257 Park Ave. S., NY, NY 10010, for a brochure about recycling many items—including batteries. Then share this information—along with your own ideas—with the class.

FACT 9

About 240-260 million tires are discarded every year.

 Find out what tire dealers in your city do with used tires. Also find out if your city has any specific place to dispose of or recycle old tires. Write the results of your investigation and mail them to the local newspaper.

 With a partner, research how rubber is recycled. Then come up with a list of ideas for using old tires throughout the school and community.

FACT 10

The 1988-1989 Annual Report of the Environmental Defense Fund said, "Other industrial countries produce one half as much trash per person as [Americans] do, and recycle a major portion of it...."

 Work with others to find out what countries like England and Japan are doing to eliminate garbage by recycling. Then report your findings to the class.

 As a class, plan a recycling event for the next PTA meeting by drawing posters and banners, holding demonstrations, and raising money by selling things such as "garbage" jewelry and sculptures. The goal of the event, of course, should be to get parents more involved in recycling.

ROBOTS

FACT 1
Around the year 250 B.C., an inventor named Ctesibus is said to have built statues that drank water.

★ Make a timeline of early automatons, leading up to Elektro and his robot dog Sparko, which Westinghouse promoted at the 1939-1940 New York World's Fair.

★ With a partner, plan and tape record an interview between a reporter and computer scientist. In the interview, explore the similarities and differences between these early automatons and computerized robots.

FACT 2
Robots can easily go to places where people would have problems—such as Mars.

★ Write and illustrate an article for a news magazine that covers the landing of *Viking I* on Mars in 1976.

★ Create a bulletin board that explores all of the other extraordinary places where robots have gone—such as the bottom of the ocean to find the Titanic. Add labels and captions with important information.

FACT 3
The word robot was invented in 1920 by a Czech writer who wrote a play about robots that were supposed to improve life on earth but ended up destroying it.

★ Create a photo essay that shows the popularity of robots in science fiction films—such as *2001: A Space Odyssey* and the Star Wars series.

★ Work with others to write, rehearse, and perform a short play about robots in 2500.

FACT 4
Robots do things that would be dangerous for people—such as washing tall buildings or painting bridges.

★ In an oral report, tell about these and other similar uses of robots.

★ Create a picture essay that explains how robots are also used in hospitals and farms.

FACT 5
Most modern robots work in factories. In fact, soon a factory in Japan will open that will use robots to make robots.

★ Draw and label a diagram that shows how a jointed-arm factory robot works.

★ With a partner, plan and hold a debate about the pros and cons of using robots instead of people in factories.

FACT 6

Mobile robots can navigate by having maps programmed into them.

Create a mobile that highlights the different ways that mobile robots are presently used and could be used in the future.

Pretend you are the inventor of mobile robots. Hold a press conference in which you explain the biggest problem with mobile robots and how that problem can be solved.

FACT 7

Without a program to tell it what to do, a robot could no nothing at all.

Work with others to plan and hold a panel discussion on the four different ways to program a robot.

Give an oral report that explains how future robots—equipped with artificial intelligence—will be different from present robots.

FACT 8

Some robots now can "feel" and "see" what they are doing.

Create a filmstrip that shows all the new things robots with sensors can do. Then record a narration to go along with it.

Write a chapter for a children's science book that simply explains how sensors work in robots.

FACT 9

Weapons designers are working on robots that could take front-line positions to limit loss of human life in future wars.

Create a series of cartoons that illustrate ways that robots may some day be used outside of the home.

Write an editorial to your local newspaper in which you voice your opinion about robots and explore whether they will ever totally replace people in the workforce.

FACT 10

Joseph Engelberger, known as the father of robots, is developing a home robot named Isaac—after Isaac Asimov.

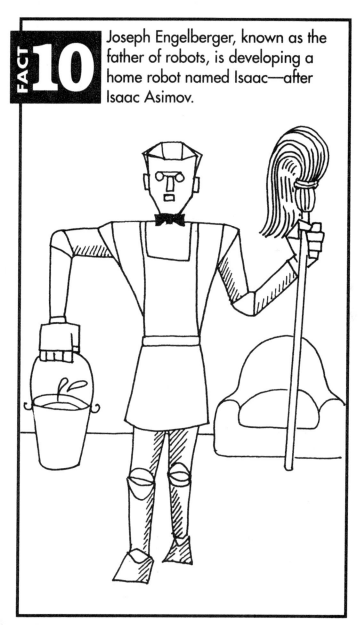

Write and illustrate a booklet that describes all the things that a robot might be able to do in the home.

Write a book report about one of Asimov's books about robots called *I, Robot* or *The Best of Robots*—or any other fictional account of robots.

ROMAN EMPIRE

FACT 1 According to legend, Rome was founded in 753 B.C. by two brothers, Romulus and Remus, who were the sons of the war god Mars.

⭐ Re-tell the myth that explains the origins of Rome. Then be prepared to give a dramatic oral presentation of the myth to the class.

⭐ Create a timeline that includes the major events in the history of the Roman Empire from its creation in 753 B.C. to A.D. 476 when the last emperor lost his power.

FACT 2 The colosseum in Rome is a marvel of Roman engineering. For example, it was designed so that its 50,000 occupants could get out of the building in a few minutes.

⭐ Make a model of the colosseum and then be prepared to explain to the class how it was constructed.

⭐ Prepare a calendar of events for the Roman Colosseum, including a brief description of each one.

FACT 3 Some Roman emperors went mad with power. For example, Nero is blamed for starting the great fire of Rome in A.D. 64 so that he could build himself a new capital.

⭐ Pretend you are a reporter for the Roman Times in A.D. 64. Write a complete report on the fire that destroyed much of Rome.

⭐ Work with others to present an oral report about the various Roman emperors.

FACT 4 At the height of the Roman Empire in the 2nd century A.D., a total of about 150,000 foot soldiers belonged to the Roman army. They were divided into Leigons—about 5,000 soldiers per legion.

⭐ Pretend you are a Roman foot soldier in the 2nd century. In a series of diary entries, write about your life—including everything from why you joined the army to what your clothes and weapons look like.

⭐ Create a bulletin board that illustrates the various duties of the Roman soldiers during both wartime and peacetime.

FACT 5 The Romans were great builders. They invented the dome, developed concrete, created aqueducts that supplied water to the cities, and built roads and bridges that are still standing today.

⭐ Draw a layout of what Rome might have looked like in the 2nd century. Include all major buildings—like temples and amphitheaters—and all public areas like the forum and burial grounds.

 Create a film strip that explains how Roman bathhouses were heated. Then record a narrative to go with it.

FACT 6 Augustus, Julius Caesar's adopted son, became Rome's first emperor in 27 B.C., and Rome continued to be ruled by emperors for the next 400 years.

 Write and illustrate a biography of Augustus.

 Write and illustrate a chapter for a children's history book that explains the period of time between 509 B.C. and 27 B.C. when Rome was a republic.

FACT 7 An ancient Roman recipe calls for mice cooked in honey and poppyseed; another calls for song birds served in an asparagus sauce.

 Pretend you are a rich Roman during the 2nd century. In a letter to a friend, describe in great detail a dinner party you had.

 Pretend you and a classmate are poor Romans during the 2nd century. Write, rehearse, and present a conversation in which you both complain about the available food.

FACT 8 Across the Roman Empire, people worshipped hundreds of different gods, goddess', demigods (half gods), and spirits.

 Prepare a *Who's Who of Roman Gods and Goddesses'* by naming and describing some of the prominent Roman gods. Include the proper sacrifices for each one of them.

 Pretend you are a modern historian. In a magazine article, explain why the Romans presecuted Christians from time to time.

FACT 9 Very few Romans lived to be more than about 50 years of age.

 Pretend you could go back in time and interview a Roman citizen to find out the major causes of illness and death and the Romans' attitude and reaction to them. With a partner, plan and write out the interview.

 Give an oral report that explains how Romans buried the dead.

FACT 10 By A.D. 395, the Roman Empire was divided into two states: east and west.

 Work with others to hold a panel discussion that explains the causes for the decline of the Roman empire.

 Plan an educational TV show that explains the different fates of the eastern and western empires.

SEA LIFE

FACT 1

Weighing as much as 25 tons, the whale shark is the world's largest fish.

⭐ Create a board game that singles out the trend setters of the fish world; for example, feature the biggest, smallest, the ugliest, the most unusual, etc.

⭐ Create a mini dictionary of sea life that shows the great variety of kinds of fish. Include pictures with captions that name the fish and give interesting information about each one.

FACT 2

An ocean sunfish can lay 300 million eggs in one year.

⭐ Create a picture essay that shows the unusual ways that some fish parents—like the South American cichlid and the Coelacanths—take good care of their young.

⭐ Write a story that tells what would happen if every egg that the world's fish lay actually hatched. Then at the end, explain the reasons why all the eggs never hatch.

FACT 3

To lay their eggs, European eels will journey up to 4,000 miles nonstop across the Atlantic Ocean.

⭐ Plan a TV program for PBS that follows the eels on their incredible journey. Also include what happens to them after they lay their eggs.

 ⭐ Create a slide show that shows how salmon also make harrowing journeys

back to the rivers where they were hatched to lay their eggs. Then record a narration for it.

FACT 4

Flashlight fish have tiny bacteria under their eyes. These bacteria give off enough light to read a watch by.

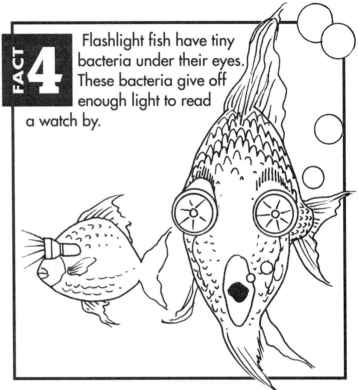

⭐ Give an oral report that explains the purpose of the light of the Flashlight fish. Then explore the broader topic of how all fish actually see and hear.

⭐ Write a chapter for a children's science book in which you give interesting examples of the great ability fish have to adapt to their surroundings and to protect themselves.

FACT 5

The lungfish of Africa can sleep outside of the water for an entire summer.

⭐ Pretend you have just been to a new aquarium. Write a letter to a friend of yours in which you explain how lungfish and mudskippers are able to breathe outside of the water.

☆ Draw a diagram that explains how most fish breathe through their gills. Then explain your diagram to the class.

FACT 6 The arapaima is an extraordinary fish because it has remained relatively unchanged for over 350 million years.

☆ Pretend you are an arapaima. In your fish journal, write a series of entries that tell about your daily life.

☆ Write and illustrate a book called *Strange Sea Life*. In your book include pictures and descriptions of other extraordinary fish—such as the Glass Catfish and the porcupine fish.

FACT 7 Some starfish have as many as 25 arms.

☆ Write a dictionary entry that defines "echinoderms," a group of animals that the starfish belongs to, and then give some characteristics of echinoderms.

☆ Create a poster that explains how echinoderms are different from mollusks. Show examples of both groups.

FACT 8 Sharks have no bones in their bodies. Their teeth and skeletons are made of a tough tissue called cartilage.

☆ Pretend you are a shark. Write an editorial that protests the bad reputation of all sharks. Then explain how sharks may some day help medical researchers find a cure for cancer or AIDS.

☆ Create a Wanted Poster for the red piranha fish that is much more deadly than any shark.

FACT 9 The blue whale is the largest animal in the world—even larger than any of the extinct dinosaurs.

☆ Write and video tape a public service announcement for TV that describes the blue whale and explains why it is almost extinct. Then explain what can be done to reverse this trend.

☆ Pretend you are a third grade teacher. Prepare a lesson that explains why whales, unlike fish, sometimes might hold their breath for more than 2 hours. Use visual aids for better understanding.

FACT 10 Electric eels and electric rays stun their prey—sometimes with enough electricity to kill a horse.

☆ Create a film strip that shows the unusual ways that some fish catch their food. Then record a narration to go with it.

☆ Create a mobile that shows the food chain—start with the smallest fish and work up to the great blue whale.

SPACE TRAVEL

FACT 1
With the Russian launch of *Sputnik* on Oct. 4, 1957, the Space Age was born.

⭐ Pretend you are Dwight Eisenhower, who was President at the time. Write a speech that you would have given to the American people to explain the position of the U.S. regarding the beginning of the Space Age.

⭐ Create a mobile that explains what a satellite is and that illustrates some of the different jobs that satellites perform today—such as weather forecasting.

FACT 2
On April 12, 1961, Yuri Gagarin, a Soviet cosmonaut, became the first human to go into space. Less than one month later, on May 5, 1961, Alan Shepard became the first American to go into space.

⭐ Pretend you are Alan Shepard. In a series of journal entries, write about your experiences during this flight.

⭐ Give an oral report on the competition to conquer space that existed between the Soviet Union and the U.S. in the 1960s and 1970s. Include the reference to this competition that John F. Kennedy made in his inaugural address in 1961.

FACT 3
On March 18, 1965, Soviet cosmonaut Alexei Leonov became the first person to walk in space. On June 3, 1965, Ed White became the first American to walk in space.

⭐ Draw diagrams that show the differences between White's walk through space and astronaut Bruce McCandless's walk through space in 1984.

⭐ Create a bulletin board that shows some of the products that Americans use today that were originally developed for the space program.

FACT 4
On June 31, 1966, the Russians landed the *Luna IX* probe on the moon.

⭐ Create a timeline that highlights the early lunar probes—both Russian and American—and within captions explain what they accomplished or what was learned from them.

⭐ Pretend you were the head of NASA in the 1960s. Write a report that explains the early failures of the lunar probes.

FACT 5
On July 16, 1969, American Neil Armstrong became the first person to walk on the moon. His total time on the moon was 21 hours, 36 minutes, and 21 seconds.

⭐ Draw a storyboard that shows Armstrong's activities on the moon.

☆ When Neil Armstrong took his first step on the moon, he said, "That's one small step for man, one giant leap for mankind" (he meant to say 'a man', but "swallowed" the 'a'). Write an essay that explains what you think he meant.

FACT 6
On March 3, 1972, *Pioneer 10* was launched. After making a 620-million-mile flight past Jupiter, it became the first man-made object to escape the solar system.

☆ Write a series of press releases from scientists at NASA that reveals what they learned about the outer planets as Pioneer 10 passed each one of them and sent back pictures and information.

☆ Work with others to plan and video tape a debate on the possibility of life on another planet. Base your arguments on information that is known about the planets.

FACT 7
On May 14, 1973, the 100-ton *Skylab*, America's first and only space station, was placed into orbit.

☆ Prepare a picture essay on various projects conducted in *Skylab*.

☆ With a partner, plan a debate. One person should take the position that a new space station is needed, and the other should take the position that Americans' tax dollars would be better spent on something else.

FACT 8
On Oct. 18, 1989, a probe called *Galileo* was launched. When it reaches Jupiter in 1995, it should be the first probe to travel through 400 miles of Jupiter's stormy atmosphere.

☆ Pretend you are a NASA scientist. Write a report that explains what NASA hopes to learn through the *Galileo* probe to Jupiter.

☆ Write an editorial that argues for or against the continuation of the space program.

FACT 9
On June 18, 1983, Sally Ride became the first American woman to orbit the earth.

☆ Read aloud some of Ride's descriptions of the earth during her flight—such as Single Room, Earth View. Then explain what you think the earth might look like from the same vantage point in the year 2500.

☆ Write a front-page news story about Jan. 28, 1986, the day that the *Challenger* shuttle exploded shortly after liftoff, killing Christa McAuliffe and 6 other astronauts.

FACT 10
On April 12, 1981, the American space shuttle *Columbia* was launched. It was the largest craft ever to go into orbit.

☆ Pretend you were a TV news reporter in 1981. In your pre-liftoff coverage, explain how differently *Columbia* will return to the earth—compared to all previous spacecraft. Include illustrations.

☆ Make a chart that compares the accomplishments of the various *Columbia* missions.

SPORTS HISTORY

FACT 1
The marathon began in 490 B.C. after a fully armed Greek soldier ran 24 miles to Athens to report a military victory. After announcing, "Rejoice! We have won!", he collapsed and died.

⭐ Create a timeline that includes the dates and descriptions of the rest of the history of the ancient marathon.

⭐ Pretend you are a television reporter covering the famous Boston Marathon. Plan what you would say before the race begins to inform your viewers of the background of the modern marathon. Then video tape or record your report.

FACT 2
The very first baskets used in basketball were peach baskets attached to the balcony of a gymnasium.

⭐ Pretend you are Dr. James Naismith. In a series of journal entries, explain why and how you created the game of basketball.

⭐ Create a bulletin board that tells the story of the famous Globe Trotters basketball team.

FACT 3
In the Middle Ages, field hockey was once outlawed in England because it interfered with archery training, which was needed for the national defense.

⭐ With a partner, plan an interview between a sports writer and a field hockey player. Discuss all aspects of the sport—including its history.

⭐ Create a chart that illustrates the differences between field hockey and ice hockey. Include famous players in both sports.

FACT 4
The first bases used in baseball were 4-foot high stakes. However, when so many players were injured when they ran into them, the stakes were replaced with rocks, but they were also hazardous and were finally replaced by bags filled with sand.

⭐ Write a newspaper article for the sports page of your local newspaper that exposes the myth that Abner Doubleday created baseball.

⭐ Create a board game that features and describes some of the early equipment and rules of baseball.

FACT 5
American football actually evolved from two English games: soccer and rugby.

⭐ Work with others to plan, write, and video tape a TV quiz show called Football Mania. During the program, contestants should be quizzed about the history of football.

⭐ Research the history and present status of your local football team or your favorite football team. Then write and illustrate a promotional brochure about the team.

FACT 6

There is evidence that surfing actually began in prehistoric times.

 Create a time capsule that includes items that reflect the long history of surfing. Label each item with all important information.

 Write and illustrate a booklet for beginners that explains how to surf safely.

FACT 7

Badminton is not an offshoot of tennis—as so many people think. Actually, this separate sport began in India centuries ago.

 Through a series of drawings with captions, relate the history of badminton.

 With a partner, demonstrate the rules for badminton.

FACT 8

The bow and arrow began as a weapon.

 Write and illustrate a chapter in a book about the origins of different sports. In your chapter, cover the history of archery.

 Think of as many peaceful uses of bows and arrows as you can—create a poster that illustrates and explains them.

FACT 9

Bowling began in 5,200 B.C.

 Write the words for a poem or the lyrics for a rap song that recounts the history of bowling.

 Create a catalog that features and describes some of the early equipment used in bowling.

FACT 10

The first blades for ice skates were made by grinding down bones.

 Write and illustrate a booklet that gives pointers to beginning skaters.

 Give an oral report on figure skating as an Olympic event. If possible, show some video segments of actual figure skating competition.

THE SUN

FACT 1

As recently as 400 years ago, men were put in jail for believing that the sun was the center of the solar system. Not until Nicholas Copernicus came along in the 16th century did this belief became widely accepted. As a result, Copernicus is known as the father of modern astronomy.

⭐ Create a storyboard that explains how Copernicus came to be known as the "the father of modern astronomy."

⭐ Pretend that you are Copernicus. Write about your life in a journal.

FACT 2

The sun—with its family of planets—moves in an orbit around the center of the Milky Way at approximately 140 miles per second. Since it takes the sun about 230 million years to complete one orbit, the sun has circled the center of the Milky Way only about 20 times in the 4.6 billion years since it was formed.

⭐ Pretend you are an astronaut traveling through the Milky Way. Describe in a report what you see.

⭐ Create a futuristic travel brochure about a trip from the earth to the sun. It should include factual information about the sun and the Milky Way.

FACT 3

Skylab was the first manned space station to study the sun, in 1973-1974.

⭐ Create and label a timeline that shows the various findings of Skylab.

⭐ Pretend you are a former astronaut. Write a speech that urges members of Congress to support a new—even bigger—space station.

FACT 4

Residents of North America will not see another solar eclipse—a time when the moon directly aligns itself in front of the sun and hides it—until the year 2017.

⭐ Pretend the time is 2017 and you have the opportunity to see the next solar eclipse. Write your impressions of it in your journal.

⭐ Create a government brochure that explains solar eclipses. It also should instruct people on things they should and should not do during a solar eclipse.

FACT 5

Scientists think that the sun has enough fuel to shine for 5 billion more years.

⭐ Pretend you are the sun's mother. Write a letter to the universe that explains the many wonderful benefits of your "son."

⭐ Write a futuristic story that tells what happens to the earth as the sun starts to lose its strength. Although the story is fictitious, it should be based on actual facts about the sun.

FACT 6

The sun is 93,000,000 miles from the earth. If you flew there at the top speed of a 747 jumbo jet, you would not reach the sun for 17 years.

⭐ Give an oral report on the harmful effects of the sun's rays. Begin your report by retelling the story of Daedalus and Icarus.

⭐ Work with others to write, rehearse, and video tape a TV commercial for a new brand of sun screen. Include the reasons why sun screens are important.

FACT 7

The energy released by one large solar flare could meet all of the earth's energy needs for the next 100,000 years—IF the earth's energy needs never increased and IF scientists could capture and transport that energy.

⭐ Write a myth that explains solar flares and the enormous energy they release.

⭐ Write a letter to NASA in which you argue for the need for an invention that would capture the energy from solar flares for use on the earth. NASA's address is 400 Maryland Ave. S.W., Washington D.C. 20546.

FACT 8

The sun is the most abundant renewable energy source available on the earth today.

⭐ With a partner, write a debate that stresses both the advantages and disadvantages of replacing fossil fuel and/or nuclear energy with solar power.

⭐ Make or draw a model of a solar powered house. Then explain how it works to the rest of the class.

FACT 9

The sun is only one of the more than 2000 billion stars in the Milky Way.

⭐ Draw and label a diagram that shows the main constellations in the Milky Way that can be seen from the earth.

⭐ Write a chapter for a children's science book that explains what is known about solar systems in the nearest galaxies: Andromeda and the Magellanic Clouds.

FACT 10

Not enough sunlight on the earth may have caused the extinction of the dinosaurs.

⭐ Draw a cartoon strip that explains this theory about the extinction of dinosaurs.

⭐ Hold a panel discussion on some of the other theories that try to explain the extinction of the dinosaurs.

TEXAS

FACT 1
At the Battle of the Alamo, Mexican President General Antonio López de Santa Anna defeated the Texans, including Davy Crockett and James Bowie.

☆ Pretend you are Santa Anna. In a series of journal entries, explain why you attacked the Texans at the Alamo.

☆ Write a section for a children's history book that explains what happened later in 1836 between Santa Anna and another group of Texans along the San Jacinto River.

FACT 2
Sam Houston, who defeated Santa Anna, became the first president of the Republic of Texas.

SAM HOUSTON

☆ Write a brief biography of Sam Houston, including the time he spent living with the Cherokee people.

☆ Create a timeline that includes all the major events that occurred during the 10 years that Texas was a republic.

FACT 3
The Texas Rangers were one of the most colorful, efficient—but deadly—bands of men on the side of law and order that the world has ever witnessed.

☆ With a partner, plan and tape record an interview with a Texas Ranger back in the late 1830s. Explore how the Rangers lived and some of the famous battles they fought.

☆ Pretend you are a Texas Ranger. Write an editorial for a local newspaper that explains why the Texas Rangers came into prominence in the late 1830s.

FACT 4
Mexican President Santa Anna warned that if Texas joined the Union, his country would go to war with the U.S.

☆ With a partner, write a debate between two Texans back in the early 1840s. One should want Texas to become a state, and the other should want Texas to remain an independent republic.

☆ Write and illustrate a brochure that covers the history of your state before it became a part of the Union.

FACT 5
Long before the first Europeans set foot in Texas, several Native American tribes lived in the area.

☆ With a partner, plan and act out a modern day press conference. One of you should pretend to be a descendent of the Karankawa people, who lived along the coast, and the other a descendent of the Caddoes, who lived in what is now East Texas. Both of you should tell about your tribes before the Europeans arrived.

★ Create a time capsule of things that show the different aspects of the lives of the Native Americans who lived in what is now your state. Label the importance of each item and explain why you included it.

FACT 6 The Comanche and Kiowas eventually moved into what is now Texas to hunt for buffalo.

★ Create a film strip that shows how Native Americans hunted and captured buffalo. Then record a narration to go with it.

★ Create a poster that shows how Native Americans used every part of a killed buffalo.

FACT 7 In the 1800s, some Texas ranchers measured their land in "RI's," or "Rhode Islands." Because the ranches were so huge, Texans were the first Americans to develop branding.

★ Create a board game about cattle rustling, including some of the unusual brands that were used in the early days of ranching.

★ Write and illustrate a children's book about the life of a Texas cowboy in the 1800s.

FACT 8 In 1936, in the middle of the nation's worst depression, Texas spent millions of dollars to celebrate the centennial of its independence from Mexico.

★ Pretend you are a Texan in 1936. In a series of journal entries, write about your experiences at the centennial.

★ Write a newspaper article that describes the centerpiece of the celebration, the 1.2 million dollar Hall of State Building.

FACT 9 Today Texas is the second largest state in area (after Alaska) with a population of over 17 million people.

★ Create a mobile that highlights ways in which Texas leads all other states—in areas such as cattle, sheep, and cotton. In captions, include statistics and other important information.

★ Pretend that you are the governor of your state. Give a speech that explains what makes your state outstanding today.

FACT 10 Millions of tourists spend over 2 billion dollars annually in Texas.

★ Write a travel brochure for Texas, focusing on all the major attractions, like its two national parks. Include a map and pictures.

★ Pretend you are the head of your state's tourist bureau. Create and video tape a TV commercial that features the special attractions in your state.

U.S. DISASTERS

FACT 1 More than 10 million gallons of oil were spilled into Prince William Sound, Alaska, on March 24, 1989.

 Write an article for a news magazine that covers this oil spill. Include pictures and captions.

 Write a follow-up story that emphasizes the clean-up, the trial of the ship's captain, and the efforts being made to prevent future spills.

FACT 2 On Jan. 28, 1986, the *Challenger* space shuttle exploded 73 seconds after liftoff, killing all 7 crew members.

 Pretend you are the head of NASA. Write a report to the President that explains the circumstances before the explosion, that describes the explosion, and that proposes the possible cause.

 Work with others to debate the importance or lack of importance of the manned space program.

FACT 3 On March 28, 1979, radioactive material was released after a partial meltdown in one reactor at the 3-Mile Island Nuclear Power Station near Harrisburg, PA.

 Pretend you are a reporter for a local Harrisburg TV station. Video tape the report you would have given that day about the nuclear accident.

 Research and present to the class the pros and cons of nuclear energy. Then preside over a class discussion.

FACT 4 On May 25, 1979, all 272 passengers aboard an American Airlines DC-10 were killed when the plane crashed after it lost its left engine upon takeoff from Chicago.

 Pretend you were an eye-witness to this crash. Write the account of this tragedy that you would have told the federal investigators.

 Create a bulletin board that describes and explains all the advances in safety that airlines have made since 1979.

FACT 5 On April 10, 1963, 126 people died when the atomic-powered submarine *Thresher* sank in the North Atlantic.

 Pretend you were the top ranking admiral in the Navy at the time of the sinking. Write a report to the President explaining what happened.

 Give an oral report that explains what future problems might result if nuclear waste leaks into the ocean.

On one day, March 18, 1925, tornadoes were responsible for 792 deaths in Missouri, Illinois, Indiana, Kentucky, Tennessee, and Alabama.

⭐ Pretend you are a reporter for a radio station in one of the 6 states hit by the tornadoes. Tape record—as if you were reporting over the radio—a description of the tornado as it passed through town. Then tell about the destruction it left behind.

⭐ Pretend you are a weather forecaster for your local TV station. Explain what causes tornadoes and why they can cause so much damage and so many deaths.

Throughout 1918, influenza (also known as "the flu") killed over 500,000 Americans.

⭐ Write a section for a children's science book that explains what influenza is and tells why so many died back in 1918. Also explain why influenza is no longer such a threat.

⭐ With a partner, write an interview between a reporter and the U.S. Surgeon General on a modern epidemic that has taken many American lives in recent years. Also explore what is being done to eliminate this new threat.

After a coal mine explosion on Dec. 6, 1907, in Monongah, West Virginia, 361 miners died.

⭐ Pretend you are a reporter for the local newspaper. Write your account of this tragedy. Include personal stories of local families.

⭐ Make a chart that lists the advantages and disadvantages of using coal as a source of energy. Then rate coal against nuclear energy and other sources of energy.

On Aug. 27-Sept. 15, 1900, over 6,000 people died from the effects of severe winds and a tidal wave as a result of a hurricane in Galveston, TX.

⭐ Create a picture essay that explains what causes hurricanes and tidal waves and that reveals their power. Include important information in labels and captions.

⭐ Give an oral report that explores why, with radar and warnings, the death toll due to a hurricane will never be as high in future.

On May 31, 1889, the worst flood in American history killed more than 2,200 people in Johnstown, PA.

⭐ Tape record a guided tour of Johnstown the day after the flood. Explain not only the cause of the flood but also describe the destruction that it caused.

⭐ Create a bulletin board that illustrates the damage done to cities along the Mississippi River during the flood of 1993.

U.S. GEOGRAPHY

FACT 1

Although Canada and the U.S. are about the same size, the population of the U.S. is almost 10 times more than Canada's.

⭐ Create and illustrate a chart that highlights the similarities and differences between the U.S. and Canada in areas such as land use, climate, industry, natural resources, and history.

⭐ Write and illustrate a chapter for a children's book that tells the history of the St. Lawrence Seaway, a joint project of the U.S. and Canada.

FACT 2

Death Valley in CA has the lowest elevation in all of the U.S.

⭐ Plan a show-and-tell with pictures that features the interesting plants and animals that exist in harsh environments like Death Valley.

⭐ Create a board game that includes information about Mt. McKinley in AK, which is the highest point in the U.S. at 20,320 feet above sea level. Include its history and its current importance.

FACT 3

The Appalachian Mountains in the eastern U.S. were formed between 280 and 300 million years ago. The Rocky Mountains in the western U.S., however, were formed "only" 60-80 million years ago.

⭐ Create a film strip that explains the three ways that mountains are formed. Then record a narration to go with it.

⭐ Draw and label a physical map of the U.S. and create a color scale that can be used to determine the heights of all land surfaces.

FACT 4

The Mississippi River is the longest river in the U.S., running 2,340 miles from Lake Itasca in MN to the Gulf of Mexico.

⭐ Draw a map that traces the route of the Mississippi. Mark and label all the industry along the river that is dependent upon it.

⭐ Create a picture essay about another famous U. S. river like the Rio Grande or the Colorado River.

FACT 5

The Hawaiian Islands consist mainly of the tops of a submerged volcanic mountain chain.

⭐ Give an oral report that explains the ways in which volcanoes have positively affected the economy of the Hawaiian Islands.

⭐ Write and illustrate a travel brochure of the Hawaiian Islands, highlighting the many differences in birds, animals, climate, etc. between the islands and the mainland, which is 2,016 miles away.

FACT 6

The Great Salt Lake in Utah is 75 miles long and 15-25 miles deep, and it is the second saltiest lake in the world after the Dead Sea.

⭐ Write and video tape a TV commercial for Utah's Great Salt Lake and the surrounding area.

⭐ Write and illustrate a section of a children's geography book about another U.S. lake— such as Lake Superior, which is the second largest lake in the world after the Caspian Sea.

 FACT 7

In 1988, 6 million acres of U.S. forest were destroyed by fire.

⭐ Pretend you are a fire fighter. In your journal, write about the causes of forest fires and new ways of controlling them.

⭐ Work with others to develop a new fire prevention campaign for Smokey the Bear. Include billboards, magazine advertisements, and TV commercials.

 FACT 8

Since their formation 10,000 years ago, the Niagara Falls have eaten their way 7 miles up stream. If the erosion continues at this rate, the falls will disappear into Lake Erie in 22,800 years.

⭐ Create a bulletin board that explains how water is such a great source of erosion.

⭐ Create an illustrated diagram that explains how falls like the Niagara are used to produce hydroelectric power.

FACT 9

Puerto Rico, which Columbus discovered on his second voyage to America in 1493, is an island that is only about 100 miles long and 35 miles wide.

⭐ Write and illustrate a leaflet for the Tourist Bureau that tells the history of Puerto Rico.

⭐ Pretend you and two classmates are Puerto Rican citizens. Each one should choose one of the following positions and write an editorial to the local newspaper, defending that position: Puerto Rico should become a state; it should remain a commonwealth of the U.S.; it should become independent.

FACT 10

Barrow, Alaska, is the northernmost town in the U.S.

⭐ Pretend you are the state historian. Write and illustrate a booklet that tells the history of Alaska.

⭐ With a partner, plan and video tape a debate that explores whether the natural gas and oil in Alaska should be mined or the land should remain a natural habitat for wildlife.

FACT 1

The longest rainless period in U.S. history was 767 days—Oct. 3, 1912-Nov. 8, 1914—at Bagdad, CA.

★ Pretend you are the weather reporter for a local TV station. Plan a presentation for an elementary school in which you explain the difference between weather and climate. Also tell about the different factors that affect climate. Include visual aids.

★ Create a slide show about making rain by seeding clouds. Then tape record a narration to go with it.

FACT 2

During a severe windstorm, the Empire State Building may sway several feet in either direction.

★ Write and illustrate a weather glossary that defines the two regional kinds of winds known as chinook and Santa Ana. Include explanations of how they affect weather in the western part of the U.S.

★ Investigate wind patterns where you live by attaching a stamped postcard with your school's name and address on several helium-filled balloons. On the card, ask the person who finds the card to write when and where it was found and to mail the card to you. Then release the balloons on different days. When you get the cards back, mark on a map when and where each balloon was found. Then report your findings to the class.

FACT 3

Places with a tropical wet climate—such as Hawaii—have the most predictable weather on the planet. It rains nearly every afternoon.

★ Give a demonstration that shows how air masses affect the weather.

★ Investigate the climate in your town by contacting the local U.S. Weather Bureau. For example, find the average maximum and minimum temperatures for each month; the averages for rainfall, snow, and sleet; and the average wind speeds for different months. Make a chart of your findings and then report them to the class.

FACT 4

The lowest recorded temperature in the U.S. was -79.8 F at Prospect Creek Camp, Alaska on Jan. 13, 1971, and the highest was 134 F at Death Valley, California, on July 10, 1913.

★ Create a poster that shows the differences between Fahrenheit and centigrade or Celsius. Then explain your poster to the class and tell about the background of both systems.

★ Check the high and low temperatures in your area and then make a chart that compares them to the highs and lows of major cities throughout the U.S.

FACT 5 Studies in modern China have found that one can predict weather with 80% accuracy by monitoring the croaking of frogs.

⭐ Call your local radio or television station or the U.S. Weather Bureau and arrange to interview a meteorologist to find out what his/her job consists of. (Plan your questions before the interview.) Then tape record your interview and play it for the class.

⭐ Plan a picture essay that shows all the different means that U.S. meteorologists use to predict the weather. Include important information in labels and captions.

 FACT 6 All of the 5 warmest years in the past 130 years occurred around the globe in the 1980s.

⭐ Check with the local weather bureau to find out any trends and/or changes in temperatures over the past 20 years. Then make a graph with your findings and explain what you learned to the class.

⭐ With a partner, plan a debate in which one person takes the position that the greenhouse effect is causing the earth to warm, and the other person refutes this theory.

 FACT 7 The highest wind velocity ever recorded in North America was measured on Mount Washington in New Hampshire on April 12, 1934, at 231 mph.

⭐ Plan a show-and-tell that explains why changes in temperature make the air move.

⭐ Create a bulletin board that uses the Dust Bowl of the 1930's as an example of the power of wind to erode the land.

FACT 8 The greatest one-day snowfall in the U.S. was 75.8" in Silver Lake, Colorado, on April 14-15, 1921.

⭐ For a weather dictionary, write and illustrate entries that cover the different kinds of winter precipitation.

⭐ Pretend you are the head of the Dept. of Transportation in your town. Write a report to the mayor in which you explain the problems caused by using salt to de-ice roads in winter, and suggest other methods.

 FACT 9 At 50,000 F, lightning's "return stroke" is hotter than the surface of sun, which is 11,000 F.

⭐ Write and illustrate a booklet for the U.S. Weather Bureau that explains what causes lightning and what to do to protect yourself during a period of lightning.

⭐ Pretend you are Benjamin Franklin. In a series of journal entries, write about your experiences with lightning.

 FACT 10 In one day, a hurricane can release enough energy to power the whole U.S. for 6 months.

⭐ Draw a storyboard that shows the development of a hurricane. Include captions to explain each box.

⭐ Pretend you are a radio announcer in one of the cities hit by Hurricane Andrew in 1992. Write the script of what you would have reported, and then tape record your report.

VOLCANOES

FACT 1

There are about 600 active volcanoes on the face of the earth today.

★ With a partner, plan a TV show for PBS that covers some of the positive aspects of volcanoes. Then video tape your show, including as many visual aids as possible.

★ Pretend you are Vulcan, the Roman god of fire. In a dramatic monologue, tell about your life and explain why volcanoes were named after you.

FACT 2

Although Mt. Lascal, in the Andes Mountains, is the highest active volcano in the world at 18,077 feet, it is still shorter than Mt. Everest at 29,028 feet.

★ Out of molding clay, make models of the three different kinds of volcanoes. Then explain their differences to the class. Also point out which kind of volcano Mt. Lascal is.

★ Pretend you are a geologist. Write a report for the National Geological Society on the different kinds of rocks that are formed from volcanoes, including the kind Mt. Lascal produces.

FACT 3

Oregon's Crater Lake, which lies at the top of an extinct volcano, is the second deepest lake in North America.

★ Write and illustrate a tourist brochure that explains how Crater Lake was formed. As a part of your explanation, include a labeled cross-section of the volcano.

★ Create a bulletin board that explains the differences among active, dormant, and extinct volcanoes. Include pictures and examples of each kind.

FACT 4

Centuries after Mt. Vesuvius erupted in AD 79, archaeologists dug up the Roman city of Pompeii—just as it was that day. For example, they found a bakery that still had bread in the oven.

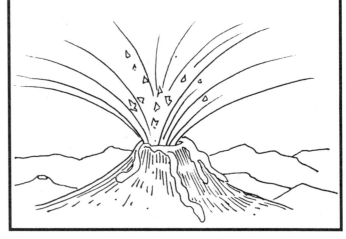

★ Pretend you are one of the early archaeologists who discovered Pompeii. Write a report that includes some of your most astounding findings.

★ Pretend you were a survivor the eruption of Mt. Vesuvius. Write a letter to a relative that tells the events of that day and explains how you survived.

FACT 5

Mt. St. Helens in Washington had been dormant since 1857 when it erupted on May 8, 1980.

★ Pretend you were a radio announcer near Mt. St. Helens when it erupted. Write and tape record what you might have said to your listeners that day to describe what you were seeing.

⭐ Write a newspaper article that describes the damage and destruction caused by the eruption of Mt. St. Helens.

⭐ Write a guide for tourists at the Moon National Monument. Illustrate your guide with maps and pictures.

FACT 6 The eruption of Krakatoa in the East Indies in 1883 sent ash 50 miles into the atmosphere, and the ash circled around the earth many times.

⭐ Pretend it is the summer of 1884, and you are a newspaper weather reporter. In your weekly column, explain the cause for 1884 being called "The Year without a Summer."

⭐ Pretend you work for the National Weather Bureau. Hold a press conference in which you explain how the eruption of Mt. Pinatubo in the Philippines on June 9, 1991, affected U.S. weather in 1992.

FACT 7 In 1980, David A. Johnston, a volcanologist, was killed during the eruption of Mt. St. Helens while he was studying the volcano.

⭐ Pretend you are David Johnson before the eruption of Mt. St. Helens. In a series of journal entries, explain what you do as a volcanologist. Include how much people like you are able to predict volcanic eruptions.

⭐ Prepare a leaflet for new residents of Washington State on how to live safely in the shadow of a volcano.

FACT 8 Apollo astronauts trained at the Moon National Monument in Idaho before they traveled to the moon.

⭐ Pretend you are the director of NASA. Write a memo to the President explaining what the Moon National Monument and the surface of the moon have in common.

FACT 9 Yellowstone National Park in Wyoming has more active geysers than all of the rest of the world put together.

⭐ Pretend you are a forest ranger at Yellowstone. Write the speech you would give to tourists that explains the connection between geysers and volcanoes.

⭐ Draw a diagram of a geyser and with captions and labels explain how it is like an underground tea kettle.

FACT 10 All of the Hawaiian Islands were created from volcanic eruptions.

⭐ Work with others to write and act out a one-act play that explains the Hawaiian folktale about Pele.

⭐ Draw a map that highlights how the Hawaiian volcanoes are a part of the famous Ring of Fire that goes along the perimeter of the Pacific Ocean.

WATER

FACT 1

About 70% of the earth's surface is covered by water.

★ Draw a flat map of the world that labels all of the major bodies of water. Then explain to the class how prehistoric people and animals could have crossed from Asia into North America.

★ Create a board game that is based on facts about bodies of water throughout the world. An object of the game might be stopping pollution in the rivers, lakes, and oceans of the world.

FACT 2

Rainwater is harmful to your health if it is acid rain.

★ Write and illustrate a chapter for a children's science book that explains how acid rain is produced and what kinds of damage it causes.

★ Write a newspaper article that explains what countries like the U.S. and Canada—as well as environmental groups—are doing to stop acid rain.

FACT 3

Of all of the water in the world, 97% of it is in the oceans. A little over two-thirds of the remaining fresh water is frozen in the glaciers of Greenland, Antarctica, and the high mountain regions.

★ Write and illustrate a children's book about glaciers. Explain how they are formed and what happens when they move.

★ Pretend you are the captain of the *Titanic*. Before the ship becomes submerged, write in your log what happened and explain why a ship that was supposed to be unsinkable was actually going to sink.

FACT 4

Some 1.2 billion people in the world today do not have access to safe drinking water. In fact, approximately 365 people die every hour—every day—as a result of drinking contaminated water.

★ Create a bulletin board that clearly illustrates different sources of water pollution as well as some possible solutions.

★ Write a story—based on facts about humans' need for water—about a town that discovers one day that all of the groundwater for miles around is unsafe to drink.

FACT 5

It is easier to float in salt water than in fresh water.

★ Demonstrate to the class how a hard boiled egg sinks to the bottom of a jar filled with tap water but floats to the top if salt is added. Then explain why Fact 5 is true.

★ Give an oral report that explains the cause of salt water. Then tell about the technology for changing salt water into drinking water.

about conserving water. Then turn your information into a series of conservation posters to hang around the school.

FACT 6
The Grand Coulee Dam, on the Columbia River in Washington State, is the greatest power producer in the world.

 Pretend you are a resident of Washington State. Write an editorial to your local newspaper in which you argue that Washington—as well as other states—needs to consider alternative sources of power such as wind power and solar power.

 Create and illustrate a chart that clearly explains the various uses of dams. Also include their advantages and disadvantages.

FACT 7
20 to 50 inches of dry, powdery snow, when melted yields just one inch of water.

 Create a mobile that features the different shapes that snow flakes (crystals) can take. Also include an explanation of how they are formed.

 Snow makes up only 7 of the 10 kinds of frozen precipitation in the international snow classification systems. Plan a show-and-tell that explains the other 3 and how they are formed.

FACT 8
If you leave the water running while you brush your teeth, you will waste about 5 gallons of water. That is enough to fill about 50 soda cans.

 Write and video tape a public service announcement for TV that highlights tips for conserving water in the bathroom and kitchen.

 Write to Ecological Water Products, 1341 West Main Rd., Middletown, RI 02840, and ask for a catalog and information

FACT 9
Every summer about 270 billion gallons of water are used up each week— just to water lawns. That is enough water to give every person in the world a shower for four days in a row!

 Pretend you are a reporter for a local TV station. Write and video tape a news report on tips for watering lawns and alternatives to watering.

 Work with a group to plan and hold a panel discussion about ways—besides watering grass—that millions of gallons of water are wasted every year in your home, your school, and your community.

FACT 10
More than 100,000 marine animals—including seals, whales, and dolphins—die every year from consuming garbage (especially plastic) and pollution in the seawater.

 Write and illustrate an environmental leaflet that covers the causes and solutions of so many of these deaths.

 Pretend you are a dolphin. Write a letter to the people of the world, asking them to stop polluting your home.

NOTES